Genetic Engineering

Also by Carl Heintze

Circle of Fire: The Great Chain of Volcanoes and Earth Faults
A Million Locks and Keys
The Priceless Pump: The Human Heart
Search Among the Stars

GENETIC ENGINEERING
Man and Nature in Transition

by

Carl Heintze

publishers since 1798

THOMAS NELSON INC.
NASHVILLE / NEW YORK

First Edition

Library of Congress Cataloging in Publication Data

Heintze, Carl.
  Genetic engineering; man and nature in transition.
  SUMMARY: Discusses the importance of genetics in the balance of nature and recent research concerning man's influence on the control of genes.
  Bibliography: p.
  1. Genetic engineering—Juvenile literature.
[1. Genetics] I. Title.
QH442. H44   573.2'1   74-959
ISBN 0–8407–6376–X

1809252

For my grandchildren
as yet unborn
with the hope
they will be

Acknowledgments

My special thanks to Stanley Skillicorn, M.D., chief of neurology at Santa Clara Valley Medical Center, and David H. Walworth, M.D., president of its medical staff, who read this book in manuscript and suggested several corrections. Any errors, however, are mine, not theirs. I would also like to thank my daughter, Jane, who helped type it, and my editor of long association, Mrs. Gloria Mosesson, for her continued help and encouragement in both this and other endeavors.

Contents

Part I
The Making of Man

1

A Delicate Balance

When white men crossed the Great Plains to California in the last century, they had to climb the Sierra Nevada Mountains before they could reach the Pacific Ocean. On the mountains' western slopes, extending in a belt for more than sixty miles, they found groves of huge trees, *Sequoia gigantea*, and when they reached the West Coast, they found the great redwood trees, *Sequoia sempervirens* —the tallest living things on earth. Many feet thick at their base, both types of conifers tower as high as three hundred feet into the sky. They are also very old. The rings in their wood show that many of the redwoods sprouted more than two thousand years ago and the sequoias in the Sierra Nevada Mountains sprouted more than three thousand years ago. Only the bristlecone pines of the White Mountains to the east along the California-Nevada border are older. Thus sequoias have been growing on the western slopes of the mountains for centuries, the only break in their long and stately procession the gaps left by the glaciers of the last Ice Age.

The size and beauty of the trees have made them objects of great interest and admiration for thousands of visitors. They also are important to science. Few communities of living creatures and plants have survived in a well-balanced state of natural harmony for such a long time.

Ecologists—those who study groups of living creatures and plants and their relationship to each other and their environment—call such a community a *climax community*, a term intended to show that it has reached the highest possible state of natural development. In such a collection of life forms the balance between the forces of nature and the various species may remain unchanged for years, even centuries.

Nature seems to strive constantly toward a climax state, but seldom achieves it, and then only for a brief period. The sequoia groves, however, have been able to live with the plants and animals around them longer than almost any other community of life on earth. Only with the coming of man has their balance been disturbed.

Not long after the discovery of the sequoias lumbermen began cutting them down to obtain wood for houses, fence posts, grape stakes, wine barrels, and other projects demanded by a rapidly growing California. Years passed before it became clear that unless something was done, the trees would become extinct. The sequoias were unable to reproduce themselves as rapidly as they were being cut. To save the trees that remained, laws were passed closing the groves to timbering. Next came the creation of national parks. Sequoia, Kings Canyon, and Yosemite National Parks now include most of the largest trees that still remain. Within the parks no one may cut the trees. In addition, camping is permitted only in designated campgrounds, and no fires are allowed near the sequoias. These measures were intended to restore the groves to their climax state—that is, to make it possible for the trees to reproduce themselves at a rate equal to their death.

Like all conifers, sequoias propagate by dropping ripened cones from their boughs to the ground beneath. There the cones break open, spilling their seeds onto the ground, where they germinate and grow rapidly into seedling trees. Each sequoia drops many cones, producing many seedlings. Few, however, reach maturity. Snow, not enough sun, other trees, lack of moisture—all these can kill the sprouting trees. Sequoias must also compete with other conifers, expecially the Douglas fir, which thrives under the shade of sequoia branches. Nature compensates for the loss of seedlings, however, by dropping many more cones and seeds than are needed, and for centuries the trees were able to propagate successfully at a rate that ensured the continued survival of the forest.

The coming of man changed all this. Not only were the groves reduced by logging; closing them to fires also deprived the sequoias of a natural cleansing agent. Scars on the trunks of the largest trees show that periodically in the past their ranks were swept by wildfires, most of them probably started by lightning. But now men prevented or fought wildfires and allowed no man-made fires to be set. Year after year the trees rained down dead needles, boughs, and cones until a layer several inches thick, called *duff*, covered everything around their trunks. As cones fell from the trees, they struck the duff and their seeds scattered, but the thick, spongy layer prevented the seeds from reaching the ground and germinating. Naturalists studied the problem and suggested to the National Park Service that experimental small plots of the sequoias be cleared and burned. The trees could then drop their cones and seeds on the bare ground, where moisture and sunlight would permit germination. The first experimental burnings proved successful, and additional acres of the park floor are now being cleared in an effort to grow more sequoias.

Whether this will restore the forest to its former natural climax state is not certain, however, for man's mere presence has disrupted it in other ways. The largest sequoias are so popular that they are visited by thousands of people each year. The pressure of many feet on the sequoias' shallow wide root system has already caused irreparable damage to their underground system for obtaining nourishment. While footpaths and paved roads are now being diverted away from the trees, some trees may already be lost. Other man-made factors, as yet undiscovered, may also have had unmeasured effects on the forest.

Although long-lasting climax communities in nature are few, they show man two important things—if he will heed the warning: First, his interference in natural communities is almost always disruptive and often fatal. Second, life in almost any form seems forever to be striving toward a climax state.

Not only does nature seek to maintain a balance between the members of a natural community but also to maintain a balance between the various processes within a living creature. This process works even in man. Each human being is a highly organized living system. The basic unit in that system is the living cell. Although cells perform different functions, depending on whether they are in the brain, liver, skin, heart, or elsewhere, they are all a part of the larger system, which is the human body. Life within the body seeks a balance, and this process is called *homeostasis*. As with climax communities of nature, when the balance is not maintained, the system may die. Of course, this balance is not static. The body, its cells, and its systems constantly undergo readjustment. Work and rest, disease and health, inspiration and expiration—all are counteracting forces moving toward a balance. We work only to rest; we inhale only to exhale; we get sick only to get well.

Homeostasis is one of the measures of life, and it helps to define what life is. A rock, for instance, is not homeostatic, but inert.

A rock also lacks another important quality of life—the ability to reproduce itself. Living matter, whether single-celled or organized into a complex system of cells as varied as the human body, must be able to reproduce itself. Cells are the simplest unit of life, and when most of them reach a certain size, they reproduce. If the cell were to grow larger, it would be unable to sustain its life. Therefore, it must reduce in size if it is to remain in balance. A cell usually reproduces by dividing, a process called *mitosis*. However, some cells reproduce by uniting with another cell to make a single new cell. This process is known as *sexual reproduction*, because it can take place only when the two cells involved are male and female. Both processes are necessary for the existence of life on earth.

All life must have a third quality, too—the ability to adapt to the surroundings, or environment, in which it finds itself. Only living forms can adapt. Inert matter cannot change itself to fit its environment. Rather the environment changes it. A rock may be ground into sand as it is tumbled about in a river, but the rock itself does not order this change. The ability of living forms to adapt to their environment, to find their individual *niche* in their own ecological community, is another reason why life has survived on earth. Faced with constantly changing conditions in the dynamic world of the biosphere, that thin film of gases and water that covers the earth's surface, life has constantly had to adapt to a changing environment. The ability to evolve with time into new forms, or as ecologists call them, *species,* has made it possible for life to continue on this planet for three billion years.

Man has known about evolution for a little more than a hundred years. From 1831 to 1836 a young British naturalist, Charles Darwin, sailed around the world on board H.M.S. *Beagle,* which stopped at the Galápagos Islands off the west coast of South America. The Galápagos are a group of many small islands and about fifteen large ones, which were formed when volcanoes appeared above the sea and then became dormant. Each island is populated with a variety of birds, plants, and reptiles, which must have come to their new home from elsewhere, for no life could have appeared until after the eruption of the volcanoes. Although the Galápagos' species seem once to have been similar, they now have many different variations, depending on the island on which they evolved. Darwin found this fascinating. As he wrote in his diary of the voyage:

> I never dreamed that islands about fifty or sixty miles apart and most within sight of one another, formed precisely of the same rocks, placed under a quite similar climate, rising to a nearly equal height, would have been so differently tenanted.

Long afterward, when he had returned to England, Darwin's observations formed the inspiration for *On the Origin of Species,* one of the famous books of history. In it Darwin proposed that life has survived continuously since it first appeared on earth, but that in order to do so, it has constantly changed, or *evolved*, to fit the earth's changing conditions. Darwin took a long time to announce this idea publicly, in part because he wanted as much scientific proof as possible, but also because he knew the effect his theory of evolution would have once it was made public. In the end he was forced to do so because another English scientist, Alfred Russel Wallace, then living and working in the Far East, had reached almost the same conclusion at about the same time. The Darwin-Wallace theory ran counter to most of the thinking of the late nineteenth century. Then most men in the Western World thought of man as a unique creature, created in God's image, placed on earth by him, and inspired by divine will to rule the world. This view was based on a literal reading of the opening chapters of the Old Testament:

In the beginning of Creation, when God made heaven and earth . . . God said, "Let the waters teem with countless living creatures, and let birds fly above the earth across the vault of heaven. . . . Let the earth bring forth living creatures, according to their kind." . . . So it was. God made wild animals, cattle, and all reptiles, each according to its kind; and he saw it was good.

Then God said, "Let us make man in our image and likeness; to rule the fish in the sea, the birds of heaven, the cattle, all wild animals on earth, and all reptiles that crawl upon the earth. . . ." (Gen. 1:1–26, New English Bible.)

Thus the Bible indicates that God made man and other forms of life at the same time and gave man dominion over all other creatures. Wallace and Darwin thought otherwise. They contended that life passed through many different forms before man finally emerged as life's present dominant species. Although they agreed with the biblical description of man as the highest form of animal, they knew from many different discoveries that his arrival on earth was recent and that his rule, far from dating from the beginning of the world, was only a few thousand years old. Darwin was also influenced by a British geologist, Sir Charles Lyell, who, in turn, was influenced by James Hutton, a Scot. Hutton, in particular, had studied the layering and shifting of ancient rock beds and had found that they were millions of years old. Within some of the oldest rocks were fossils of ancient sea creatures, but nowhere among them could the remains of any ancient man be found.

Man's beginnings came at a much later time in the earth's history, during the emergence of primates. The family of primates includes not only man but also monkeys, apes, chimpanzees, and baboons. All of these animals are superficially similar to man—they can walk erect and have skulls, jaws, fingers, and skeletons much the same as ours. Yet they are significantly different too. Their backbones form only a single curve, while man has a double curve to his spinal cord; their lower jaws are larger, and their brains are much smaller; their ability to use their hands is limited.

No direct lineage, no certain connection, between man and other primates has ever been found. The search for this "missing link" has occupied *anthropologists,* the scientists who study man, since Darwin's time. It has both confused and encouraged the quest for proof of the time when man emerged as a separate species. Gradually, many scientists have come to believe that man appeared suddenly as himself in the world, rather than evolving slowly from other older species of primates.

The uncertainty about man's early life on earth is partly due to the fact that few clues to his early existence have been found. Bone fragments of creatures like man have been found in widely scattered parts of the world, in Africa, Indonesia, China, Europe, even the United States, but the skeletons of these early creatures are not like those of any primates of today, including man.

The earliest yet known remains are those of a small creature called *Australopithecus,* "southern ape," who lived in the Cape Province, South Africa, about a million years ago. The australopithecines may have walked erect, and they almost certainly lived off other animals, perhaps even others of their own kind, but anthropologists still cannot agree as to whether they were the forefathers of *Homo sapiens,* the species to which man belongs.

In 1959 the late Dr. L. S. B. Leakey discovered in the Olduvai Gorge in Tanzania a massive skull with very large teeth, which he named *Zinjanthropus boisei,* a type of australopithecine. Pebble tools found nearby seem to indicate that these cave dwellers were indeed human.

Another species of primate, the pithecanthropoids, lived in Indonesia and China about half a million years ago. They were larger and more powerful than the australopithecines and probably eventually drove them into extinction.

About seventy-five thousand years ago the pithecanthropoids were succeeded by the earliest variety of our own species: first, *Neanderthal man,* named for the Neanderthal Valley in Germany, where the remains were first discovered; then *Cro-Magnon man,* named after a cave in France where the bones were found; and finally, Homo sapiens as we know him today.

During this long period of evolution, man did not rule the world as he does now, but shared it with many other species, and he did not live in a world like the one we know today. While he was evolving, the earth was periodically overcome by great sheets of ice, which inched down over most of the Northern Hemisphere. As with man himself, the reasons for the coming of ice are not known, but either during one of the Ice Ages or in the warm interval between two of them, man—Homo sapiens —appeared. How and why he happened to evolve then also remains a puzzle, but somehow he managed to survive, despite both the cold and the many larger and better-protected warm-blooded animals that then inhabited the earth.

Life in those early days cannot have been pleasant or easy. Man was a migrant, in search of warmth, shelter, and food. He lived by killing creatures smaller than himself, although now and then he may have banded together with others of his kind to trap and kill larger animals too. As he struggled for survival, he underwent an explosive transformation—a transformation so rapid it is without parallel elsewhere in the earth's history. His head suddenly grew larger to make room for a brain three times the size of any other primate's. As he developed this greatly enlarged brain, man achieved a quality that no other species possesses: He learned to think abstractly, to store knowledge, and to communicate it to his fellows through speech. No other animal has the power of speech, and no other species has the ability to use thought in an abstract way. Man became what Dr. Loren Eiseley, a noted scientist and writer, has called a dream animal, a creature capable of forming, storing, and using ideas, rather than simply reacting to the basic animal drives of sex, hunger, and thirst.

In addition to acquiring his larger brain, man developed differently from other animals in another way. His larger brain needed a larger skull, a skull too big to pass through his mother's birth canal. Therefore, it had to grow gradually through an infancy and extended childhood far longer than that of any other species, often as long as seventeen years altogether. For such a prolonged infancy and childhood, man needed permanent parents—anthropologists call it *pair-bonding*.

Permanent relationships between males and females seldom occur in other species. Most males and females mate for a single season, and once the young have been raised and weaned, sometimes even before that happens, the mates part and are seldom reunited. Such a condition was impossible if man was to survive to adulthood. He needed a permanent family in which to grow and parents from whom he could acquire knowledge.

The creation of a permanent family made possible collective, rather than individual, searches for food and shelter, and increased man's ability to compete with other species. With a family and with new knowledge, man was able to discard many of the characteristics required by other species. He no longer needed hair all over his body for warmth; nor did he require special physical modifications in order to hunt and kill. Instead, with his growing fund of knowledge, he learned how to make tools for specific tasks, tools that could be changed as the need arose.

Another mystery of man's development is why it took him so many centuries to develop weapons and utensils.

For thousands of years he seems to have had nothing more than sharp or rounded stones, although even they, when used as clubs, cutting tools, or scrapers, were something no other species had. Perhaps stone tools were adequate for the needs of early men, who seem to have had plentiful supplies of other animals on which to depend for food. Whatever the reason, the use of more complicated tools does not appear in man's history until about ten thousand years ago, when the last Ice Age abated and the earth warmed. Then the second explosive development in man's evolution took place.

Suddenly, within a few centuries, men began to settle down and become farmers. They had discovered agriculture. As with other important parts of man's story, no one knows why. One conjecture is that as the ice receded from the earth and its climate warmed, it was no longer hospitable to many species on which men had come to depend for food—species that had evolved in a cold climate and could not adapt to the change. Species after species disappeared, and man's plentiful supply of meat dwindled. Men may then have had to turn to plants for food. They may have first harvested only wild plants, but it did not take them long to discover that they could grow increased supplies of cereal grains by planting them.

The planting of crops, the beginning of agriculture worked important changes in the way man lived. It meant he could now settle in a single region, rather than wandering as game wandered. Settling down may also have involved religion—some scientists think so. Whatever the cause, the collection of men into farming communities suddenly produced here and there cities and then nations. In the Nile Valley in Egypt, in central Mexico, in China, and in the Middle East, men began to gather together in fertile valleys, often near rivers, to plant the earth, to plan and build cities, to invent writing and number systems, to develop social order, to create religion, and to emerge into the light of recorded history.

This process, the gathering, storing, and transmission of man's accumulated knowledge, did not begin everywhere at once, and it has not yet happened everywhere in the world, even today. Over a period of eighty centuries, civilizations rose and fell as first one group of men and then another applied its own set of solutions to the problem of living together. In some places the transition from the Stone Age to agriculture took from six to ten thousand years. In others it is only now being completed. In parts of Africa, Asia, and South America, each one a continent where history first dawned, men have lived for hundreds, perhaps thousands, of years only a step beyond the beginning of civilization. There men still cut and burn the jungle and forest, still crudely plow the nearly barren earth, and still plant barely enough to feed themselves. They still draw water from communal wells, have few domesticated animals, and cannot yet read or write. Only slowly are they being drawn by the more developed parts of the world into man's third great evolutionary step— industrialization.

For the rest of the earth the agricultural era has passed and been replaced by a technological revolution. Beginning in Europe in the eighteenth century, the Industrial Revolution spread quickly to the New World and then across the Pacific to Japan, now one of the most industrialized nations on earth. The Industrial Revolution has meant the construction of more and more machines to do man's work, more and swifter means of communication and transportation, and the use of ever more complex tools to increase the amount of work that men can do. An industrial society is often measured by the number of factories and cities it has, but technology's first great effect on man was to free him from constant working of the land to grow food. As man learned to use machines, he was able to grow more, and as he grew more, he could feed more.

Industrialization has also had another important effect. It has forced man into an ever more specialized and compartmented life. Where once a single man could perform all the work needed to raise enough food for himself, now many men are required to grow much more. One man alone can farm, but will raise little. One man equipped with a tractor can grow more, but it takes many men to build, fuel, and service a tractor. The man who runs the tractor has one skill and devotes it to farming, but the men who build the tractor, the men who mine the ore from which its metal parts are fabricated, the men who fashion the parts and assemble them, those who drill for oil, refine it into fuel, and distribute it to farmers, all have learned jobs far removed from growing crops. They are dependent on the farmer to feed them, and he is dependent on them for the tractor with which to do the job.

None can work without the help of the other, and neither farming nor manufacturing can be carried out without the pooling of many skills and much shared intelligence. Thus industrialization is a merging of men's minds as important as man's first understanding that agriculture would free him from living only as he found food from day to day. Without industrialization, man would not have come to dominate his planet as he has. Without its power, he would still be at the mercy of natural forces. A simple example is the change from sailing ships to steamships. When men depended on sails to cross the ocean, they moved only as the wind moved. The discovery of steam power and the construction of steam engines freed sailors from the whims of the wind and allowed men to move their ships as they, rather than the weather, dictated.

Of course, man is still not free of natural forces. He still must contend with storms, flood, droughts, and earthquakes, but even these may eventually come under his control. It is a measure of man's confidence today that he believes he may someday alter the weather, control or at least predict earthquakes, and prevent floods and droughts by storing natural supplies of water.

Man is now moving toward the creation of a collective world intelligence, the *noosphere*, as it has been called by a French philosopher-scientist, the late Pierre Teilhard de Chardin. The central question before man, however, is not whether this is possible, but whether it will be the salvation or the potential destruction of man. In dominating nature, is man also destroying it?

Almost everywhere in the world that man has imposed industrial power, he has been both disruptive and wasteful of the earth. An example is man's domination of the Great Plains of the American Middle West. Less than two hundred years ago the plains were a climax community built around the relationship between the American bison, or buffalo, and the vast grasslands on which they grazed. The only men in that ecological community were the Plains Indians, who killed some buffalo for food, clothing, and shelter, but did little to disturb the natural forces within the community. Their demands on the buffalo herds were not large enough to disturb the balance they enjoyed with other life on the plains.

Then, as in the sequoia forests, new invaders appeared from the east—the immigrants from Europe, who had crossed the Atlantic and the mountains and valleys beyond the Mississippi River in search of new land. The new white settlers were not hunters, as were the Indians; instead they were farmers seeking new places to grow crops. As they came, they slaughtered—in less than two decades —thousands of buffalo, forever destroying not only this species of life, but effectively wrecking the balance of the plains community. Well aware of what was happening, the Plains Indians fought the new settlers in a series of brave but futile wars, only to surrender finally and enter virtual imprisonment on reservations set aside for them in little-used and fallow portions of the plains. As for the buffalo, had it not been for the salvaging of a few of them, also to be kept on reservations, they would have become extinct.

The new dwellers on the prairies quickly converted them to farmlands, plowing up the naturally fertile grass and sowing the land with wheat, corn, and rye. Without its protective grass cover, the topsoil of the plains began to blow away in a series of great dust storms during the 1930's. Only the building of check dams to halt erosion, contour plowing, and the withdrawal of some of the land from agriculture halted the destruction of the plains.

The lesson of the Great Plains, the sequoia forests, and a thousand other disrupted, damaged, and destroyed ecological communities of the past is that man in large numbers is the most destructive natural force in the world. Man is a part of nature. Although he often speaks of it as if he did not belong to it, he cannot stand outside nature or its forces. He can modify, change, control, and destroy portions of the biosphere, but he cannot escape the consequences of his actions. The biosphere has a limit. Like all ecological communities, it is finite. It contains only so much water, air, fuel, nutrition, and life—all things that man needs for his continued survival.

Long ago, when men were far fewer in number than they are today, when they used little of earth's stores of energy, polluted few of its streams and lakes, killed few of its other species, and tilled none of its acres of land, they lived in balance with the biosphere. Since then, by increasing the production of food, and by learning through medicine to control or end disease, man has also increased his numbers so rapidly that he has thrown the natural world out of balance. At his present rate of growth he may soon effectively destroy the earth's resources, not only for himself, but for many other species as well. Man then will face the dilemma that has threatened all other dominant species in the earth's long past: If he is unable to strike a new balance with other life, he will perish in large numbers, perhaps completely, just as did the dinosaur, the woolly mammoth, the saber-toothed tiger, and the dodo bird. He will have been tried by evolutionary forces and found wanting. He will become extinct.

Fortunately, man has one great weapon in his struggle for survival, a weapon possessed by no other dominant species before him—his brain. With it he can think and plan for the future; he can see himself in relation to the whole earth.

Some men have already come to realize that man must fight to survive. They have already begun to grapple with the problem, not of making over the world to fit man, but of making over man to fit the world. Their insight makes it clear that if man is to remain dominant on earth, he must somehow learn to control himself; he must see that the secret of such control is within himself; he must reach out into other lives, not to destroy them, but to help them also remain a part of the earth. The fourth great evolutionary step for man, then, lies within himself, but also without, toward a union not only with other men, but with all life. He must make a new effort to strike a balance with a world that he has thrown badly out of harmony. Man needs to build a worldwide climax community, not only of men, but of all other life forms as well.

2

Out of the Sea

Stand on a beach in the evening and look out across the empty sweep of the ocean. Breakers roll in across the sand, dissolving into foam; they crash against the rocky headlands and fall back into the darkening sea. They are the only movement, and the seascape's only definition is the thin line where water and sky meet. The sea seems lifeless, its only hint of habitation being heaps of dead kelp and a few broken seashells tossed upon the sand by the tide. Yet if you place a drop of the sea's water beneath a microscope, you will find it teeming with life. Each cubic inch of the ocean's vast surface is filled with *plankton*—millions of tiny creatures of infinite variety, each a single cell.

The sea is life's cradle. From its reaches man traces his ancestry. Here, two or perhaps three billion years ago, the earth's first life appeared. As with all life today, it centered around a compound called *deoxyribonucleic acid* (DNA). As uncertain as the date when DNA first appeared in the seas is the question of why and how it happened. Was it by chance that the atoms of the elements that were dissolved in the earth's primitive seawaters joined together to make DNA?

The answer is lost in the past. Man will probably never know how life began, but one theory, based on experiments by Dr. Stanley L. Miller of the California Institute of Technology, is that radiant energy, either from the sun or from cosmic rays, caused atoms of carbon, oxygen, nitrogen, hydrogen, phosphorous, and other elements to come together. The energy may have also come from discharges of lightning that struck the earth. Perhaps knowing why is not so important as understanding that life was not always present on the earth, but that with the beginning of life the long thread of evolution, which finally reached man, was started.

Early life in the seas was probably not much different from the plankton that now floats in watery clouds just below the ocean's surface, gathering energy from the sun during the day and expending it during the night. Spherical, separated from the water by only a thin wall, plankton is the easiest form that life in the sea can take. The water serves to move the plankton, provide it with the elements needed for survival, protect it, and aid its reproduction.

Perhaps the early cells of life were almost transparent, even as some planktonic forms are today. They may even have contained *chloroplasts*, minute structures capable of capturing the photons of light showered on the earth by the sun and causing *photosynthesis*, or the manufacture of carbohydrates. All plant cells, including those of plant-like plankton, contain chloroplasts. Plant cells are the ultimate source of energy for all life on earth. Animal cells do not have the ability to gather solar energy through the process called photosynthesis, so animals must depend on the consumption of plants to survive. This is true for man, even as it is for all other animals. Man's life still depends on *food chains*, many of which begin in the sea. (A food chain is the consumption of one life form by another, in a successive pyramid.)

The first cells of life may have had many, perhaps all, of the structures found in living cells today. Life probably could not have continued were this not so. All plant and animal cells have a similar organization. They are divided into three principal parts: the *cell wall* (in plants) or the *cell membrane* (in animals); *cytoplasm,* the mixture of structures and substances inside the cell wall or membrane; and a *nucleus,* the directional center for the cell. Within the cytoplasm are the *mitochondria,* where energy is broken down into useful compounds; *vacuoles,* storage and digestive hollows for food brought into the cell from outside; *ribosomes,* factories for the production of molecules essential to the life of the cell; and other less well understood *organelles* such as *Golgi bodies* and *lysosomes.* All have an important part to play in the systems of the cell, as they must have had eons ago.

The nucleus of the cell is both the direction and control headquarters for such systems and the storehouse of information through which the cell is able to reproduce itself. DNA is the biochemical in the nucleus that contains this information and, it seems, the substance that orders both cell growth and reproduction. All cells contain DNA in their nuclei, no matter what form of life they represent. DNA is the same in all life, from single cells to man's highly organized collection of cells. It is a *polymer;* that is, two chains of smaller units of atoms called *nucleotides* which wrap around one another in a shape known as a *double helix.* A nucleotide consists of three kinds of substances—a base, a sugar, and phosphate. The nucleotides of DNA have *adenine, guanine, cytosine,* and *thymine* bases. Each nucleotide is similar in structure, but slightly different in its composition of atoms. DNA bases are paired; chemical bonds always link adenine with thymine, and cytosine with guanine, across the two strands of the double helix. If the two strands of DNA could be stretched flat and letters substituted for the pattern of the bases, the molecule's "code" could read:

AGCTAGCTAGCTAGCTAGCT   (first strand)
TCGATCGATCGATCGATCGA   (second strand)

The sequence of the four bases is important because somewhere within the pattern the information the cell needs for all its functions, including its own reproduction, is coded. In *mitotic cell reproduction*—where cells multiply by dividing—DNA unravels its two strands, much as one might pull a piece of twisted yarn apart, and sends one strand to each of the two new cells formed. Each new cell, with its separate strand of DNA, quickly draws atoms from its cytoplasm to assemble another strand along the length of the first one to form a new double helix. Again, if a single strand of DNA were stretched flat to form the code AGCTAGCTAGCTAGCTAGCT in the new cell, a second strand reading TCGATCGATCGATCGATCGA would be formed next to it and the two strands would then be bonded together.

This process is called *replication*, the preservation of the pattern of DNA from one cell generation to the next, and the knowledge of it is one of the most convincing arguments scientists possess for their belief that life has been continuous ever since the formation of the first DNA chain. Presumably, if it were possible to trace DNA's continuous replication back through time, the trail would eventually lead to life's beginning in the sea.

As mentioned in the previous chapter, cells also reproduce by a second process—sexual reproduction. In this

process cells do not divide, but are reproduced through
the union of a male and female cell. Yet even in sexual
reproduction DNA remains the replicating mechanism.
Before the union of the male and female sex cells, the
amount of DNA in these cells is reduced to one half the
amount in mitotic cells by a process called *meiosis*. In
meiosis the strands of DNA separate as they do in mitosis,
but the single strands do not bond themselves to a new
second strand. When, after meiosis, two sex cells unite to
make a new cell, the new cell contains the amount of
DNA that is in any mitotic cell. The new cell then reproduces by mitosis, dividing and redividing again and again.

The first life probably was reproduced by mitosis, although, of course, we cannot be sure. Mitosis makes reproduction possible, but it offers life a slow pathway to
change. Mitotic cells can be altered by *mutation*, the
random breaking of chemical bonds in the DNA helix,
to create small, but important, changes in the message the
molecule contains. Natural mutation probably happens
because of one or both of two events: some mechanical
break in a chemical bond or the destruction of the bond
because of a cosmic ray passing through the cell.

There is also a third possibility, *reverse transcription*.
It occurs when DNA, in a way not yet understood, receives a message, perhaps garbled and incorrect, from the
cytoplasm—a matter you can read more about in Chapter 6.

Natural mutation seems to affect only a single cell at a
time, and then only a few of the base pairings in the cell's
DNA. This may seem unimportant, yet spread over many
millions of years, such mutations must have caused gradual but significant changes in the early life in the earth's
seas.

Mutation offers life a limited chance at adaptation to a changing environment. Sexual reproduction can produce much swifter and more far-reaching changes in life forms. The number of possible base pairings in DNA is almost limitless. It grows as the length of the nucleotide chains in the molecule increases. Lower forms of life have short chains and contain limited amounts of information. The more complex life becomes, the longer are its nucleotide chains. In man they may attain thousands of pairings. Not only are the strands of DNA long, but in sexual reproduction two individual strands, one from the male and one from the female cell, can mix with one another. Thus even a single generation can vary considerably from its parent cells. Over many generations great variability for life becomes possible, and life has more opportunities to change to meet the challenges of the world around it. Very probably without sexual reproduction and the adaptation it permits, life would never have left the sea.

Before life left the sea, however, it had to undergo important changes. First, it had to develop from single-celled life forms into groups of differing and mutually supportive cells. Cells had to come together to become *organisms,* that is, collections of cells in which each group had a special function to perform on behalf of the entire organism. To do this, cells had to *differentiate* into heart, lung, liver, skin, eye, and brain cells. How cells came to change from generalized to specialized cells remains a mystery.

All cells *metabolize,* or use energy, to run their subsystems through *protein synthesis,* and differentiation must also have involved this process. Protein synthesis is

dependent on two forms of another nuclei acid—*ribonucleic acid,* or RNA. When RNA is formed, the strands
of the DNA helix spin out so that the nucleotides are
exposed, and new pairings of guanine and cytosine are
made. But adenine pairs with a new base—*uracil.* When
a sufficient number of these bases has been so assembled,
something in the DNA orders the RNA to detach from
the DNA *template,* or pattern, and move out of the cell's
nucleus to its cytoplasm. Because this form of RNA carries
the message, or code, of the DNA, it is called *messenger
RNA,* or m-RNA. In the cytoplasm messenger RNA uses
this code—the copied sequence of adenine, guanine, cytosine, and uracil—to form another sequence of bases,
thereby making a new form of RNA—*transfer RNA* or
t-RNA. Thus transfer RNA also has DNA's original message encoded in its sequence of bases.

Messenger RNA travels through the cytoplasm to the
ribosomes and becomes associated with them. With the
help of t-RNA, this complex is attracted to another group
of molecules, *amino acids.* Although there are only four
RNA bases, twenty amino acids exist in living matter, each
of them similar, yet each slightly different in molecular
pattern. While we do not know exactly how RNA bases
are related to amino acids, the relationship is specific;
that is, a certain number of RNA bases are needed to
attract a particular amino acid. Somehow transfer RNA
recognizes the appropriate amino acids and transfers them
to the ribosomes. Thus a chain of amino acids is assembled
to form what is called a *protein.* The number of proteins
that can be made by DNA, messenger RNA, and transfer
RNA is almost endless. Proteins are many amino acids in
length—dozens, hundreds, perhaps thousands. The dif-

ference of only a few amino acids or slight differences in their sequence can give two proteins entirely different biological properties.

Proteins have a large number of important tasks to do in the body. Some are *enzymes,* which promote or repress the functions of the cell. Some move out of the cell to become *antibodies,* substances able to neutralize invading foreign materials in the body, or *antigens.* Some amino acids may turn off portions of the DNA molecule itself. Some are probably concerned with the differentiation of the cell through successive generations, carrying orders from DNA to change the cell's form and function.

However cell differentiation happens, it began long ago in life's history, permitting the formation of differing, but supportive, cells into individualized organisms. No record of the earliest species remains for us to examine, for they had no bones, shells, or other protective structures, but were something like today's jellyfish. Only when life forms with bones or shells evolved could any record of past evolution be left for the present. Shell-protected creatures called *trilobites* are among the oldest fossils to be found in the rocks of ancient earth. Half a billion years ago they crawled over the sea floor, were captured in the sand by succeeding layers of material, and in the eons that followed, turned into rocks themselves. They are the oldest evidence man has of life in the sea. They are also evidence that at some point in time life changed sufficiently for some forms to move about by themselves.

Once life became capable of independent movement, it took the first great step forward in its evolution. The second came when it evolved a skeleton. The jellyfish-like sea creatures of the earth's early history had to depend on the water for support and movement. The evolution of a shell gave the successors of these species protection. Interior skeletons permitted the growth of larger and even more successful life forms. In addition to a skeleton, newly evolving fish grew jaws, freeing them from having to suck food from the sea bottom. With bony jaws fish could bite and chew. Finally, about 400 million years ago, fishes with lungs appeared, and 100 million years later the first sea creatures ventured onto land.

The continents then had no life, neither plant nor animal. The first *amphibians,* life forms capable of living both on land and in the water, may well first have been captured in tide pools along the shore or in riverbeds. The first plants to reach shore probably started as seaweeds with their roots, or holdfasts, anchored to the sea floor along the edge of the continents. There, as they evolved, they grew part of their foliage above the water. Gradually isolated from the sea, they came to sink their holdfasts into the continental soil as roots and to stand erect without the support of the water.

Once ashore, life grew into the vast array that continues to this day. No accurate count of the species, living and extinct, that have inhabited the earth has ever been made, but their number is in the millions. It was this great diversity of life and the dynamic force with which it constantly changed form that so fascinated Darwin on his voyage around the world on the *Beagle*. Although Darwin knew nothing of DNA, protein synthesis, or the other mechanics of the cell, he was able to appreciate, perhaps more fully than any other man of his time, the almost infinite variety of forms that life had taken to adapt to the earth's changing environment. In so doing, Darwin was struck by a seeming paradox: Although there were many different species of life, the number of members in individual species tended to remain fairly constant. At the same time, he saw also that individuals within a species seemed to multiply in geometric ratios. How could this happen? Darwin wondered. How could individuals multiply in geometric ratios without causing an increase in the numbers within an individual species?

Darwin's solution to the paradox was to say that many more individuals are born within a species than can survive and only those most fit to live (or adapt) do so. This process has come to be called "the survival of the fittest." Darwin also declared that the survival of the fittest in any species depends on their ability to change to meet the changes around them.

What he was unable to describe, because so little was then known about it, was the way in which this was accomplished, why it was so, and why and how characteristics were passed (or changed) from generation to generation in a species. Unknown to him and the world, even as he was writing *On the Origin of Species,* an obscure Austrian monk, Gregor Johann Mendel, was working out the laws and science of heredity—an explanation of how life forms transmit their characteristics from generation to generation. Mendel, the son of a peasant farmer, born in what is now Czechoslovakia, became an Augustinian monk at Brünn, partly for religious reasons, but also because of his interest in plants. He wanted to work in the monastery garden in his hometown. There he began experimenting with pea plants, crossing different varieties by exchanging pollen between them.

In his experiments he set out to observe seven plant characteristics through crossbreeding: the form of the ripe seeds, the color of the peas, the color of the seed coats, the form of the ripe pods, the color of the unripe pods, the position of flowers on the plant stems, and the length of the stems. In all, Mendel made 287 different crosses between 70 different plants. For example, he crossed plants with round seeds with plants with wrinkled seeds, plants with long stems with plants with short stems, and plants with yellow-colored peas with plants with green-colored peas. The next generation of plants had not a single wrinkled seed in their pods, had only yellow peas, and long stems. Mendel next planted the seeds from this generation, but did no cross-fertilization. Instead, he allowed the plants to pollinate themselves naturally. When he harvested the pods from this generation of plants, he found they contained both wrinkled and smooth seeds, both yellow and green peas, and both long and short stems. Mendel carefully counted his harvest. He found he had 7,324 peas, 5,474 of them round and 1,850 of them wrinkled, a ratio of three to one. The same ratio applied to the other characteristics Mendel had been observing.

Mendel again planted his collected seeds, allowed the plants to pollinate themselves, and harvested his crop. The plants growing from wrinkled seeds produced a generation with only wrinkled seeds, but the plants grown from round seeds continued the same three-to-one ratio of wrinkled and smooth seeds. His experiments to this point had focused on only one pair of characteristics at a time—such as wrinkled and nonwrinkled seeds, for instance. But now he mixed two or more characteristics, then three or more. The results were the same. The ratio of three to one remained.

From his experiments Mendel concluded that hereditary characteristics, which are transmitted from one generation to the next, are governed by two hereditary units, one from each of the parent cells. In addition, Mendel derived two laws, now called the *Mendelian laws of heredity:* First, when the parent's sex cells are formed, the two units in the parent's cells separate, and they are not influenced by each other. Second, characteristics are inherited independently of each other.

After all this work, it was clear to Mendel that there were characteristics that appeared from generation to generation, characteristics that were *dominant,* and that there were masked characteristics that seemed to disappear, but that might recur in later generations. Mendel called them *recessive* characteristics. Dominant and recessive characteristics, he also knew, appear in numerical ratios. Mendel did not give a name to the hereditary units that govern characteristics, but scientists who rediscovered his work called them *genes,* from the Greek word "to produce," and they gave the name *genetics* to the study of the transmission of characteristics from one generation to another.

When he completed his work in 1865, Mendel wrote and delivered a paper on his findings in Brünn and sent copies of it to scientific organizations, which uniformly ignored it. Mendel then wrote to Karl von Nägeli of Munich, Germany, one of the great botanists of his day, telling him what he had found and asking advice about how to continue his experiments. Although von Nägeli replied to Mendel, he failed to appreciate the importance of Mendel's work and did nothing to encourage it. Mendel eventually died in obscurity in Brünn, his work forgotten. Then in 1900 three other scientists, all working on their own, Hugo De Vries of the Netherlands, Karl Correns of Germany, and Erich Tschermak von Seysenegg of Austria, stumbled on Mendel's principles and tracked down his paper, and the Austrian monk finally received full credit for his discoveries. Along with Darwin's theory of evolution Mendel's studies showed how life, continuous since its creation on earth two or three billion years ago, was able to change through all that time.

The rediscovery of Mendel's work with pea plants opened the door to a host of discoveries about life: DNA, protein synthesis, and genetics. Man now had a broad outline of how he came to be where he is in the earth's history. Many gaps in the story remained—and still remain, of course. Although evolution explains how species evolve, it does not satisfactorily tell why some become extinct.

The story of the dinosaurs is an example. Dinosaurs evolved as the earth's dominant life form 100 to 200 million years ago. They were a step beyond the creatures of the sea. Living mostly on land, but occasionally in the air and sometimes as amphibians, laying eggs to reproduce themselves, they existed much as reptiles do today, with circulatory systems that needed the heat of the sun to keep their blood fluid and moving. Beginning as small creatures, they roamed the earth for millions of years and gradually evolved to enormous size with heavy coats of natural armor. Both their armor and size may have served as protective devices, but these characteristics also imposed immense demands on them for food. Then, about twenty-five million years ago, they died out—not just a single species, but the entire array of dinosaur varieties—leaving the fossils of their bones in the earth.

Mammals, a class of vertebrates to which man and other primates belong, arose to spread over the world. Unlike dinosaurs, which lay eggs, mammals evolved to carry their young within their bodies until birth, were warm-blooded with four-chambered hearts, and most important, developed stable interior body temperatures, which remained the same no matter how the climate changed around them.

Why did dinosaurs yield to mammals? Scientists have many suggestions, without agreeing that any one of them is correct. They believe climatic changes may have snuffed out all creatures unable to withstand extreme temperature changes, but that may not have been the only reason dinosaurs disappeared. They may also have simply outgrown the earth's food supply, or perhaps it was a combination of these and other factors, a warning from nature to man that those creatures that cannot adapt to change cannot survive.

Dinosaurs disappeared and were succeeded by mammals of many varieties. Yet mammalian hearts, circulatory systems, and reproductive systems were no guarantee of survival either. A large number of mammalian species failed to live beyond the emergence of man as the earth's dominant life form. Man evolved to overcome most of the problems faced by other species.

He had a mammalian heart and a constant interior body temperature, and was one of the few creatures to walk erect and to use, with great dexterity, his forelegs as hands. His eyes, in contrast to most life forms, were placed near the top of his head, and his vision was binocular. In fact, sight became one of man's valuable physical assets. Finally, he evolved with a brain unlike any other creature before him. With it he developed the ability to think abstractly, to speak and write, and, through language, to store a pool of knowledge.

Although man could outrun few other species, was weaker than many others, had a less sensitive sense of smell, and possessed other physical handicaps, these faults came to matter little, because of his brain. All creatures before man had special physical attributes that had developed out of their need to adapt to their environment. In the end none of these attributes counted as much as the ability to think and communicate. By using his brain, man could fashion tools that made up for any physical weakness of his body. By building shelter for himself, by using fire to keep warm and cook his food, by bathing to keep cool, by killing other animals and saving their skins for clothing, by harvesting crops and natural fibers, and finally, by working metals, he became largely independent of the particular environment in which he found himself.

The first men probably lived in trees for safety, but as their ability to meet enemies grew, they descended to the ground, and no doubt that is when they learned to walk erect. Their life as tree men gave them one more link with the other primates. Apes, monkeys, and chimpanzees still live in trees on occasion, but walk on land as well. It is interesting to note that in places where large primates did not evolve—in South America, for instance—men did not appear either.

With the coming of the last Ice Age, men turned to caves for protection in some parts of the world, but contrary to popular belief, not all men lived in caves. Some spent the last Ice Age along lake and river shores, building man's first shelters there of wood, rather than seeking protective hillsides, rocks, and hollows as dwelling places.

From these beginnings, wherever men were at the close of the last Ice Age, came the races of man that inhabit the world today. Although they have different skin colors and there are variations in height, weight, color of hair and eyes, facial features, and other characteristics, all men alive today, from the Aborigines of Australia to the businessmen of New York, are of the same species. Though their lives are often different, biologically they all face the same problems in survival, and they must seek the same solutions to those problems.

3

A Curious Creature

Man dominates the earth, yet what is he? It has been a bare two hundred years since this question was first asked with scientific curiosity. Since then man, the only creature on this planet intelligent enough to study himself, has asked the question many times. He still does not have a complete answer.

These are some of the things he knows: He is a single species named Homo sapiens, which, translated literally from the Latin, means "man, wise." Man is the most numerous and most recently evolved of the primates. His numbers are divided into three main races—Caucasoid, Negroid, and Mongoloid—and he is a descendant of previous Homo species that have become extinct. Mankind's genes have been pooled and mixed over the centuries, however, to produce thousands of variations in skin color, height and weight, shape of eyes, length of life, and body type. No single typical Homo sapiens exists, but if all his characteristics could be averaged, he would stand about five feet, five inches tall, weigh between 107 and 158 pounds, have room in his skull for a brain ranging in size from 61 to 113 cubic inches, and have a heart that beats seventy times a minute at rest. He would grow hair on his head, under his arms, around his sex organs, and, if a male, on his face. He would take from ten to seventeen years to reach maturity.

Homo sapiens, although he is not positive, thinks he began in Africa, spread east and north through Europe and Asia, then went across the Bering Sea into North and South America, and traveled by boat and perhaps by then-existing land bridges to Southeast Asia, Australia, and Micronesia. At first he must have been few—at the close of the last Ice Age, not more than a few million —yet today he numbers almost four billion and is increasing at a rate so rapid that this number could double before another century has passed.

Man is omnivorous; he can and has eaten almost anything, plant or animal. Not naturally a vegetarian or solely a meat eater, he can, however, survive on a diet of either meat or plants alone without ill effects. He transcends all ecological niches. Whereas other creatures of the world must confine themselves to a specific territory to survive, man can live anywhere in the world. He has walked every part of the earth's surface, from the frozen continent of Antarctica to the deserts of Africa and Asia. He is able to do so because of his fierce aggressiveness, not only with other creatures, but with himself as well, and because of his skill at adapting to any condition. The earth is his ecological niche and, sometimes he believes, perhaps the universe.

Alone among the primate species of the world, man engages in organized warfare, forming armies, constructing weapons, and fighting with himself. His ability to make war is a skill that both contributes to his dominance of the earth and threatens his existence. It is a preoccupation solely his own. Man has made war ever since he began to record his history, and he must have engaged in it even before then. He has waged war on himself for many reasons: land and food, control over territory and other human beings, political ideas, and religious domination. In the centuries of his struggle with himself, his battles have become ever more impersonal. Once he fought hand to hand. Today the artillery piece, the airborne bomb and missile allow one man to order the death of many.

Yet man remains a social animal, one of the most social of all forms of life. He alone has built cities and learned to live in them side by side with his fellows, for as a species, he tends to avoid solitude. His social concern and his ability have been great strengths, allowing him to pool his knowledge and intelligence and to work for the improvement of the many, rather than the few.

Although other forms of life band together as herds, schools, coveys, packs, and prides, none have such complex or such self-supporting social structures as man. Man's cooperation with his fellows is not simply for protection, food gathering, or reproduction, as it is with other species, but is also in the interest of culture.

Culture, written and unwritten, has existed at various levels and states of organization throughout man's history. It consists of rules, both written and understood; traditions, established and so accepted that they are learned shortly after birth; styles of life, art, music, and poetry; and a host of habits, customs, ideas, and prohibitions, most of them accepted from generation to generation. For example, most human cultures accept clothing of some kind as a social rule, and only occasionally, in the most primitive and the most advanced of man's societies, is nudity acceptable.

Like all other higher animals that reproduce sexually, man mates, often with elaborate courting rituals. Unlike other creatures, however, he considers love to be an important part of sexuality. This emotion is one of many such responses he thinks is impossible to lower animals. He considers emotion a part of personality, that set of responses that makes him different from any other person in the world. He equates personality with self, another concept apparently unknown to other species.

Other creatures may mate for a season or two, but man strives toward a lifelong mating with the opposite sex. Yet he can be sexually promiscuous. Sexual relations with many, however, are looked upon with disfavor in many of his cultures, and often this disfavor is backed by a strong sense of guilt and severe penalties. In almost all of his cultures incestual sexual relations between brother and sister or parent and child are forbidden.

Finally, man displays a curiosity about himself and the world known to no other species. He sees himself both as a part of the world and as a creature somehow detached from it, and he seeks to observe both it and himself with objectivity. This leads him to question why he is in the world, what his place is in it, and how that place and what he is will decide his ultimate fate. This curiosity about himself is one of his greatest characteristics, another one that sets him apart from all other creatures. They *exist;* he seeks to know *why* he exists. This need to know is a quest not only for himself, but for all life; it is a search that never seems quite satisfied by discovery, a search that can be found in his earliest recorded history, one that must have existed long before then. It is a part of all his attempts to explain his place in the world and of all his cultures. Often it is religious; sometimes it is based on science and philosophy; but it is always a part of man.

No other animal is so concerned with his being; no other creature bequeaths to his successors such a need for a future, such a legacy of desire to understand; in no other species is there such a need for immortality, such a need for the species and the individual to continue somehow after death. This need would not exist if man did not believe himself to be superior to all other forms of life, the culmination, the highest point to date of evolution. From the rise of Sumer, the earliest of man's recorded cultures, to modern civilization with all its machines and pooling of intelligence, man has had this concern. He has come to think of himself as both a single species and an individual and to believe he is a unique creature for which he has yet to find an equal elsewhere in the universe. This belief rests not so much on what he is able to sense of the world as it does on "something" he knows. The simplest expression of this faith is to be found in the words of the French philosopher René Descartes, who once wrote, "I think, therefore I am."

Man is certain that he thinks, that he has a mind, although he is not always sure just what this means. An equal part of this faith is that his mind, whatever it may be, is to be found somewhere in his brain, which, of all his organs, is the one about which he knows the least. Only higher forms of life have brains, and even among higher species no creature has such a well-evolved collection of nerve cells as man. The brain is a mass of cells.

The simplest of worms have central collections of nerves called *ganglia*, which respond to outside stimuli. For instance, if you touch a worm with a needle, it will shrink from the point. It is responding to messages sent to its ganglia from its skin. Yet a worm does not think the way a man does; it does not reason or seek to examine the point of the needle to see why it is sharp.

Only higher forms of life, creatures such as men, apes, whales, elephants, cats, and frogs, have evolved collections of nerve cells that can truly be called brains. All these creatures are *vertebrates*—that is, unlike worms and other lower forms of life, they have backbones to hold the mass of their bodies erect. All vertebrates possess *spinal columns*, a series of closely positioned hollow bones, or *vertebrae*, held together with softer material called *cartilage*. The *spinal cord*, which is a bundle of nerve fibers, passes through the spinal column, connecting nerves in all parts of the body with the brain. The bony covering of the spinal column serves not only to strengthen the body, but also to protect the central nervous system. The central nervous system is the most efficient and safest way yet devised by nature to gather nerve impulses, protect them, and route them to the brain. It also returns messages from the brain to the muscles for quick response to the world outside the body.

As with other parts of the body, both the central nervous system and the brain have been evolving over millions of years. In the simplest of vertebrates the spinal cord bulges out at the upper end into a simple brain. This emerging *brain stem* is a step beyond the ganglia of worms, but only a step on the way to man's brain. Neurologists call this stem the *hindbrain*, and tests they have made of its nerve cells indicate that it is the seat of the most elementary of responses to stimuli. Sometimes these responses are involuntary; that is, they seem to be made without conscious thought. Once set up by experience, they operate constantly to order such functions as heart beat, rate of breathing, and similar basic requirements of metabolism.

In man the hindbrain includes the *medulla oblongata,* an oblong extension of the spinal cord, and the *pons,* a bulblike formation that acts as a relay station between the *cerebrum* and the *cerebellum,* higher centers in the brain. The cerebellum, a mass of cells about the size of a tennis ball, is located at the rear base of the skull and controls muscle coordination.

In front of the hindbrain is the *midbrain,* which has centers that control the eyes and are connected to the *diencephalon.* Creatures that possess diencephalons can respond to a wider range of stimuli than simpler forms of life that have only a hindbrain. In man the diencephalon includes three divisions, the *thalamus,* the *hypothalamus,* and the *subthalamus.* Many of the nerve pathways in the human diencephalon order basic drives—hunger, thirst, and sexual desire, for example—but these responses are less involuntary than those controlled by the medulla. The hypothalamus in man also serves as a central message center for nerve impulses from the spinal cord, sorting them out and redirecting them to other parts of the brain.

In many creatures evolution stopped with the development of the diencephalon. Dissection of their bodies reveals small sections of hindbrain and diencephalon, but little above either of these two centers. In man, however, there has been a great explosion of nerve cells outward from the hypothalamus, a mushrooming of white and gray matter so large it fills the upper skull and all but covers the two lower sections of the brain. If the human skull is opened at its top, this mass of cells is all that can be seen, a mass that is ridged and indented to give it more surface within the confines of the head. This *forebrain,* the *cerebrum,* distinguishes man from all other animals. Few have cerebrums. If they do have one, it is vastly inferior in size and capacity to man's.

The surface of man's cerebrum, the *cerebral cortex,* consists of gray matter and is the location of brain cells responsible for man's most delicate responses to stimuli. It is the storehouse of his memory and may be the seat of his mind, if the mind truly has a fixed location. For convenience, this mass of gray matter can be divided into several different areas, the major ones being the *temporal, occipital, frontal,* and *parietal lobes.* The individual names of the lobes correspond to bones in the skull. The ridges and indentations of the cerebral cortex are called *gyri* and *sulci,* Latin words meaning ridges and fissures, respectively.

Man is born with ten billion nerve cells, or *neurons,* all he will ever possess, but his brain at birth weighs only about a third of what it will weigh at maturity. The increase in the brain's weight between childhood and adulthood is not an increase in the number of brain cells, but rather in their size. Soon after adulthood is reached, brain cells begin to die, disappearing at a rate of several hundred thousand a year, but this loss is of little importance before the arrival of extreme old age, because the brain has many more cells than are normally necessary.

Neurons, the nerve cells that make up the brain and spinal cord, are similar to many other cells in the body— that is, they have a cell membrane, a nucleus, and cytoplasm. However, they are unable to reproduce themselves, and in appearance they are much different from the generalized pictures of cells in biology textbooks. The cell membrane of each nerve cell has many long branches called *dendrites.* The largest and longest of a cell's dendrites is an *axon,* which is the chief pathway for the minute electrical impulses that the cell fires to the brain.

Some nerve cells of the central nervous system transmit impulses to the brain, receiving them from *receptor sites* in the skin, in the retina at the back of the eye, in the inner ear, along the surface of the tongue, or at various places in or near the major blood vessels. Such cells are called *afferent cells.* Other nerve cells called *efferent cells,* transmit impulses away from the brain. For instance, some nerve cells pass impulses from the brain to muscle cells to make the muscles move. Some cells also work to suppress or halt impulses. They are called *inhibitor cells.*

Nerve cells speed their electrical impulses along from cell to cell, sometimes at speeds of up to a hundred feet a second. The impulse moves much as a current flows through a copper wire, through the exchange of electrons between successive individual atoms in the axon. At the end of the cell's axon is a slight gap, or *synapse,* across which the impulse must jump before it moves to a neighboring cell. Here the movement is carried out by chemical reactions that take place at great speed. It is similar to what happens when the first pin in a row of ten pins is knocked down. The energy of the first falling pin is passed on to succeeding pins in the row until the last pin has been leveled.

While all this is clear, it is much less certain how nerve impulses are handled within the brain itself and how the brain is able to receive information, analyze it, formulate a response, and then return a signal to the appropriate part of the body for action. It is extremely difficult to observe the brain in action, protected as it is by the bony structure of the skull. Surgeons have opened the skulls of

human beings for brain surgery, and by stimulating specific areas of the cerebral cortex with small charges of
electricity, they have located the general sites for the
neurons governing certain responses. This technique can
be quite specific. It is also possible to stimulate a single
neuron with electricity, but it can give only general an-
swers about where response centers are located. Scientists still remain uncertain about where the pathways between neurons run and whether or not they are firmly
fixed or variable in pattern. They do believe it is the neuron's ability to generate minute amounts of electricity that
enables a cell to serve as part of a message route.

The ability of the brain to generate electricity was
discovered in the 1920's by Dr. Hans Berger, a German
psychiatrist. Dr. Berger placed sensitive electrodes on
the surface of the skulls of subjects. By using amplifiers,
he was able to detect and record wave patterns produced
by neuron activity. In time half a dozen or more differently
shaped waves were detected. Today they are labeled with
Greek letters to distinguish one from the other. It was
Berger's hope that the study of wave patterns would
tell something about how the brain worked. This has only
partly come to pass. Some brain-wave patterns indicate
serious brain disease, but usually the brain-wave patterns
of mentally ill patients are no different from those of
the mentally healthy.

Berger's system of studying the brain is called *electroencephalography*. It is now an accepted part of *neurology*,
that branch of medicine concerned with the nervous
system. Electroencephalography offers a general description of what is happening in the brain, but it does not
show how neurons are able to act as memory storage
banks, or how they are able to provide man with reason.

Man's ability to think must come through some kind of imprinting of neurons.

Most men are born with only a few basic nerve responses, such as sucking or crying. They must learn to walk and talk, tasks that usually take at least a year. No other animal has such a long learning period. Other animals seem to be born with brain pathways that go into automatic operation almost immediately after birth. Yet they are incapable of learning much more. Their brains simply do not have the capacity for additional information storage. Man's cerebral cortex is a reservoir into which he can pour millions of pieces of information.

How this is accomplished in the brain no one yet knows. Two general theories or models have been suggested. The first says that the brain is a kind of filing cabinet, where experience is registered and from which the brain is able to select the proper file. The second model is based on the electronic computer. A computer is much like a collection of neurons. It consists of many banks of "bits" and each bit is a tiny switch that is either "on" or "off"— that is, either charged with electricity or neutral. In the computer a bit that is turned on may represent a one; a bit that is turned off may represent a zero. The computer uses binary arithmetic to store numbers. In binary mathematics all numbers are based on combinations of one and zero. The larger the number is, the larger the number of bits that must be turned off or on to represent that number. A binary number thus may be many bits long.

The brain's neurons may operate in the same way. Some cells may be charged with electricity, others may be "off." Cells are linked by axons, providing an almost infinite number of linkages between "off" and "on" neurons. What is not well understood is how linkages between neurons are made and how the brain is able to direct incoming stimuli, received from nerve cells, to the proper place in its mass of cells. Nor is it known how specific sections of the cortex become centers for certain kinds of stimuli. Equally mysterious is why some knowledge needs to be given to the brain only once while other information must be repeated many times before it is learned, or how the brain is able to create responses for which it has never had any apparent specific stimuli.

The composition of a painting, the writing of music, and many other human creative acts usually reflect an individual's experiences, but as responses, they are often much different from the stimulation that brought them into being. It is at this point that scientific study of the brain merges with philosophy and religion. Some who study human behavior believe man is only an animal and that he responds to stimuli only as other animals do. To these persons, man's mind is only a collection of his experiences, and his behavior nothing more than the creation of pathways between neurons in his brain. Others, like Descartes, take a different view. They believe man has a mind and a soul and that he is equipped with a will and a personality solely his own.

One of the most extreme of those who believe man is only a more highly developed animal is Jacques Monod, a French biologist and author of *Chance and Necessity*. As the title of his book implies, Monod believes the creation of life and the evolution of man are the result of mere chance. Man thus is not the maker of his world, but rather its prisoner; there is no mind independent of the body and certainly no soul that exists after the body dies. In this view of life, there is no place for religion. It suggests that man, try as he will, cannot escape the modifications forced on him by the world. He, Monod says, cannot remake himself or reshape the earth; the earth is making and reshaping him.

Perhaps the answer to the riddle of the human mind is more optimistic than this. Perhaps its secret lies not in any single collection of nerve cells, but rather, as Dr. Loren Eiseley has written, in "that cloud of visions, ideas and institutions which hover about, indeed constitute, human society, but which can be dissected from no single brain."

In this view the human mind is not only what each of us possesses individually within his skull, but also the combination of all that mankind has learned since he emerged on this planet. We may indeed think and therefore know that we exist, but we may also bear within us, however minute, some part of all the long tradition of human thought from all the generations of man.

Again, as Dr. Eiseley has written, "Man is not a creature to be contained in a solitary skull vault, nor is he measurable as, say, a saber-toothed cat or a bison is measurable. Something, the rainbow dancing before his eyes, the word uttered by the cave fire at evening, eludes us and runs onward."

If this is true, the brain's actions and reactions may tell us much about how we think, move, and perform the necessary tasks of life, but no charting of brain waves, no studies of neurons, will ever carry us to the limits of the human mind. They are encompassed by all human experience, past, present, and future.

4

Unraveling the Thread

In 1885 the French chemist and biologist Louis Pasteur injected material he had taken from the body of a rabid dog into the body of nine-year-old Joseph Meister. The boy was being treated because he had been bitten by a rabid animal not long before. Pasteur gave young Joseph a series of injections of the material, weakened by chemicals, in an effort to prevent his death from rabies. Then, as today, a rabies infection, if left untreated, was always fatal. Young Joseph lived, proof that Pasteur had found an artificial way to stimulate his body to resist rabies virus.

Pasteur called his method of treatment *vaccination* because it was modeled on a similar system devised almost a hundred years before, in 1796, by Edward Jenner, an English physician. Jenner had found a way to prevent smallpox, a disease then widespread in Europe and other parts of the world, when he noticed a similarity between the sores caused by smallpox and those of a less serious illness, cowpox. He reasoned that if he used cowpox to stimulate the body sufficiently, it would become resistant to smallpox as well.

To carry out his experiment, Jenner scratched a small open wound in the skin of a boy named James Phipps and then introduced matter from cowpox sores into the wound. A few months later, after the sore had healed, he scratched a second wound in the boy's arm and placed pus from smallpox sores in the area. Normally, James Phipps should have contracted smallpox, but instead, he showed no symptoms of the disease. Jenner had found a way to prevent the disease by making the body mobilize its defenses for what seemed to be an attack of smallpox. Jenner called his method of treatment vaccination, a word taken from the Latin word *vaccinus*, meaning "of or from cows," from *vacca*, "cow." It was quickly accepted as a way to prevent smallpox and eventually led to almost complete eradication of the disease.

Jenner thought his method of treatment would work only with smallpox. He did not know, as Pasteur did, that all infectious diseases are caused by organisms too small to be seen except under the microscope, and that the same approach can be used to prevent most infectious diseases. Pasteur knew he must somehow isolate the organism that caused the infection and then so weaken it that, given in small doses, it would gradually cause the body to resist a major infection.

Pasteur's work marked one of the great turning points in man's history. It was the beginning of modern medicine. For the first time man clearly recognized the relationship between microorganisms and disease and knowingly controlled the chemistry of his body.

Pasteur's rediscovery of vaccination, however, was only part of his contribution to modern science and the remaking of man. He had been led to the rediscovery of vaccination by earlier studies of life, particularly microscopic life. Pasteur was a chemist who become interested in biology when members of the French wine industry asked him to investigate the action of yeast in wine.

Yeast, fed by the sugar in grapes, is what causes wine to ferment. Pasteur established that yeast consists of thousands of microscopic organisms that will grow if supplied with sugar for energy. From this, he deduced that life can exist not only in visible forms, but also in forms that can be seen only under a microscope.

Before Pasteur, scientists had long disagreed as to what life is and how it originates. One group held that life was created spontaneously from dead and decaying matter. The second group believed life could come only from other life. The supporters of the spontaneous-life theory pointed to the fact that flies and maggots often seemed to appear in decaying meat and similar substances, as if they had been created by it.

Pasteur—and other lesser known scientists before him—held that life could only come from other living forms. To settle the question, Pasteur had special swan-necked glass vessels built. They were designed so that air could be driven from them by boiling water in them. The shape of the vessels also permitted air to enter them again after they had been made sterile by boiling. Microorganisms collected at the point where filtration of the air began, but not beyond. No life appeared in any decaying material stored in the sterile portion of the flasks. Clearly, life in the form of microorganisms existed, and just as clearly, it could not appear in decaying and dead matter without the introduction of microorganisms. Some of Pasteur's flasks still exist in France with the material inside them still under sterile conditions and still not alive, even after more than a hundred years.

Pasteur's work drew modern biologists' attention to two assumptions they have used ever since: First, man can manipulate living chemical systems to do his bidding, and second, man's search for ways to do this must be concentrated in the smallest units of organized life.

Coincidentally, at about the same time that biologists came to this conclusion, physical scientists began to concentrate their attention on atomic structure and on the smallest organized units of matter. Thus from Pasteur's time almost to the present, scientists have been confident of man's ability to shape his own future, both within his body and in the world around him. Only in the past few years has this confidence been shaken by uncertainty as to whether man can control the far-reaching effects of his influence on nature.

Pasteur's work led chemists, biologists, and physicists into three areas of study: the cell, the molecules of living matter, and genetics, or the study of how living systems continue the passage of life from generation to generation. In each of these fields, one central question has persisted and is still without a definitive answer: What is life? For biologists, this question has brought a greater and greater interest in organic chemistry.

Organic chemists work with the kind of molecules found in living matter, while physical chemists work with the molecules of nonliving matter. Both of them use the same physical and chemical laws and the same more than one hundred elements in the periodic table of the elements. However, organic chemistry is chiefly concerned with four of the elements, those most abundant in living molecules: oxygen, nitrogen, hydrogen, and carbon.

These four elements are the most abundant ones in the biosphere, but of the four, carbon is perhaps the most important because of its *valency*. Valency is a principle discovered in 1852 by a British chemist, Sir Edward

Frankland. All atoms have valency—a measure of the number of electrons in their outer shell or ring. Electrons are minute particles that revolve around the dense inner nucleus of the atom. Carbon has a valency of four because it has four electrons in its outer ring of electrons. Other atoms may have more or fewer than this number, and some carbon atoms may also vary slightly from this number. If they do, they are said to be *isotopes* of carbon. However, the vast majority of carbon atoms have a valency of four, a fact that gives them both stability and the ability to combine readily with other atoms and themselves.

Understanding valency gave chemists their first insight into the construction of molecules of living matter. By analyzing living materials, early chemists determined that they were made mostly of many carbon, oxygen, nitrogen, and hydrogen atoms, but it was not clear how the atoms were arranged or why one molecule of living matter was different from another. A way out of the puzzle was found in 1857 by a German chemist, Friedrich August Kekulé von Stradonitz. He knew atoms must have some kind of structural arrangement in order to become molecules. He concluded that a carbon atom, with a valency of four, could share an electron with one, two, three, or four other atoms. Kekulé imagined a carbon atom to be somewhat like the capital letter C with four bonds, which represent the electrical attraction of the four outer electrons and are indicated by lines or dots, something like this:

$$-\overset{\textstyle |}{\underset{\textstyle |}{C}}-\quad \text{or}\quad \cdot\overset{\textstyle \cdot}{\underset{\textstyle \cdot}{C}}\cdot$$

A carbon atom thus could attach itself to other carbon atoms and form a chain, like this:

$$-\overset{\mid}{\underset{\mid}{C}}-\overset{\mid}{\underset{\mid}{C}}-\overset{\mid}{\underset{\mid}{C}}-\overset{\mid}{\underset{\mid}{C}}-\overset{\mid}{\underset{\mid}{C}}-\overset{\mid}{\underset{\mid}{C}}-\overset{\mid}{\underset{\mid}{C}}-\overset{\mid}{\underset{\mid}{C}}- \quad \text{or} \quad \cdot\overset{\cdot}{\underset{\cdot}{C}}\cdot\overset{\cdot}{\underset{\cdot}{C}}\cdot\overset{\cdot}{\underset{\cdot}{C}}\cdot\overset{\cdot}{\underset{\cdot}{C}}\cdot\overset{\cdot}{\underset{\cdot}{C}}\cdot\overset{\cdot}{\underset{\cdot}{C}}\cdot\overset{\cdot}{\underset{\cdot}{C}}\cdot\overset{\cdot}{\underset{\cdot}{C}}\cdot$$

As such, carbon is called a *monomer*. It could also share electrons with the atoms of other elements, if they have the proper valency. For example, a single atom of carbon could form a pattern with four hydrogen atoms, each of which normally has a valency of one, like this:

$$\text{H}-\overset{\overset{\textstyle H}{\mid}}{\underset{\underset{\textstyle H}{\mid}}{C}}-\text{H} \quad \text{or} \quad \text{H}\cdot\overset{\overset{\textstyle H}{\cdot}}{\underset{\underset{\textstyle H}{\cdot}}{C}}\cdot\text{H}$$

This combination is *methane,* or marsh gas, a molecule composed of one carbon atom and four hydrogen atoms. Carbon can also form a more complex pattern with nitrogen, hydrogen, and oxygen as in this structural formula for *glycine,* one of the twenty amino acids:

$$\overset{\overset{\textstyle H}{\mid}}{\underset{\underset{\textstyle NH_2}{\mid}}{HC}}-\overset{\overset{\textstyle O}{\diagup\!\!\diagup}}{\underset{\diagdown}{C}}\!\!\diagdown\!\!\underset{\textstyle OH}{}$$

Organic molecules are usually much more complicated, but these simple examples will show how organic chemists began to work out the structural formulas for the atoms of which living matter is made. Understanding how living molecules were put together was necessary if scientists were to learn how these molecules reacted with one another, and the knowledge eventually led men to learning how to alter such substances in the test tube, or, as chemists say, in vitro, two words which, literally translated from the Latin mean, "in glass."

Organic chemists found that by adding and subtracting individual atoms or groups of atoms they could radically change the form and function of living molecules. At first, they thought only living matter could provide them with the materials they needed to do this. In 1828, however, a German chemist, Friedrich Wöhler, had already found that when he heated ammonium cyanate, an inorganic substance, he could make urea, a chemical normally found in the kidney. A quarter century later a Frenchman, Pierre Eugène Marcelin Berthelot, experimenting with different forms of alcohol, found them similar in structure. By adding or subtracting portions of their molecular structure, he found he could create, or *synthesize,* alcohols at will. At almost the same time a seventeen-year-old British chemistry student, William Henry Perkin, experimenting with coal tars, discovered a way to make *aniline purple,* a dye that until then had been found only in living creatures. He thus founded the artificial dye industry.

From then on, in laboratories all over the world, biochemists began analyzing organic molecules to find their structure. Their work fell into two categories: (1) Some chemists tried to synthesize organic molecules, either by building more complicated substances from simpler materials or by creating organic molecules from nonorganic compounds; (2) others began to study the actions and reactions of living molecules in living creatures. For much of the nineteenth century the work of isolating and manipulating organic compounds moved more rapidly than the study of living systems.

One of the immediate results of this search was the creation of organic molecules that are not found in nature. Petroleum and coal tars, both fossil fuels, yielded a variety of such substances. The chemistry of petroleum became a specialized branch of biochemistry, and from the laboratories of petroleum chemists came many of the fractions of oil taken for granted today. Most of them were the result of distilling petroleum—heating it until, at various temperatures, its components could be removed as gases and then condensed into liquids.

Another group of chemists learned to join together the long chains of carbon atoms into organic molecules and founded the modern plastics industry. Most plastics are related to living molecules, but they have been altered by the addition of more atoms, often under pressure and heat. Plastics are easy to shape into almost any form, last almost indefinitely at normal temperatures, and often are cheaper to use than naturally occurring organic materials.

One of the most successful creations of plastic was developed by Wallace Hume Carothers, a chemist for the Du Pont corporation. Carothers, studying amino acids in the 1930's, found a way to insert extra carbon atoms into amino acid molecules and built a molecule now known as *nylon*. Nylon has such molecular strength it can be formed into a thin, very fine fiber, as strong as and cheaper than natural silk excreted by silkworms.

Understanding of reactions in living systems and of the organic molecules involved in life itself went more slowly. One problem in studying the biochemistry of life in vivo (in living organisms) lies in the isolation of individual reactions from the complicated and often interlocking parts that make up a single living organism. In an animal as large and complex as man, it is difficult to examine a single reaction without confusing it with others or without stopping life itself. In time scientists concluded that the best way to do the job was to concentrate on individual cells. Cells differ in function, but they obey the same chemical rules. This very elemental idea was first proposed in 1824 by a French physiologist, René Joachim Henri Dutrochet. A few years later, in 1838 and 1839, two other scientists, Matthias Jakob Schleiden and Theodor Schwann, revived the idea in Germany and made it basic to all biological research. In 1860 another German, Rudolf Virchow, put it in a new and final form: All cells arise from other cells. The study of life must concentrate on cells.

This assumption centered the attention of biologists on the cell, but it did not answer the basic question concerning life: What is the "stuff" of life? Is it the same in all living systems?

In 1869 another German, Friedrich Miescher, extracted and refined from white blood cells a white, sugary substance. Miescher determined it was part of the cells' nuclei, and so he called it nuclein. Later a second similar material was purified and also found to be a part of the nucleus. The first of these nucleic acids was called deoxyribonucleic acid and the second ribonucleic acid. There Miescher's discovery lay, forgotten by biologists for years while scientists instead turned their attention to the way in which cells live, or metabolize.

Human metabolism is dependent on a constant supply of three groups of chemicals found in food; *proteins*, fats or *lipids*, and *carbohydrates*. Water, oxygen, and some minerals such as copper and iron also play important roles in metabolism, but the basic groupings of food are proteins, lipids, and carbohydrates. As food enters the body, it is broken down in the stomach and intestines and absorbed into the body through the intestinal walls. Thereafter it embarks on a series of journeys along *metabolic pathways* through the organs of the body. Along the way, atoms or groups of atoms are added or taken away from the various components of food. During these complicated reactions carbohydrates are either "burned" to release their energy or stored as fat to be used at a later time. Much the same thing happens to lipids. Proteins are broken down into other substances and redistributed.

The body also makes its own protein through protein synthesis, directing some of its reactions with protein enzymes. It also can assemble protein *hormones*, although not all hormones are proteins. Protein hormones are manufactured in glands in the body and directed through the blood and lymph systems of the body to start and stop biochemical processes.

Protein hormones were the first biochemical substances in metabolism to be isolated. In 1901 Jokichi Takamine, a Japanese chemist working in the United States, separated a hormone called *adrenaline* from other human biochemicals and carefully studied it. He found it had an effect on the blood pressure. A year later two British scientists, William Maddock Bayliss and Ernest Henry Starling, discovered a second hormone, *secretin*. Secretin is made in glands on the wall of the small intestine and acts upon the pancreas gland, causing it to release digestive chemicals necessary to break down food.

A third important hormone, *insulin*, was identified in 1922 by three Canadian scientists, Frederick Grant Banting, Charles Herbert Best, and J. J. R. Macleod. They found that insulin is made by a special group of cells in the pancreas, called the *islets of Langerhans* after their German discoverer, Paul Langerhans. Persons whose islets of Langerhans do not produce adequate amounts of insulin are diabetics. They are able to live only if they receive a daily injection of insulin and eat a carefully controlled diet.

Having isolated proteins and hormones, biochemists now tried to synthesize them in the laboratory. They quickly found, however, that their molecular structures are exceedingly complicated. Not only do they contain more atoms than many organic substances, their structure also is often difficult to map. Every protein is a chain of amino acids held together by chemical links called *peptide bonds*. In addition, many protein chains are curled and curved into peculiar individual shapes, sometimes with cross-linkages between portions of their chain.

Analyzing a single protein often takes years. The peptide bonds have to be broken to separate the amino acids so the precise place of each one in the chain can be mapped. Cross-linkages must also be determined. Some molecules have a "right" and "left" hand—that is, they are mirror images of one another—and this, too, must be determined by chemists. The study of even the simplest of protein chains is a complicated matter. It is immensely difficult to study proteins such as *hemoglobin*, the substance in the blood that acts as a carrier for oxygen and carbon dioxide. Hemoglobin contains 550 amino acids. Yet it is only an average-sized protein. Others are even larger and more complicated.

By the middle of the twentieth century, it had become clear to biologists that somewhere in the body's ability to make protein lay the secret of life itself. Since metabolism is, in a sense, life, and since protein metabolism depends on the ability of the cell to synthesize protein, an understanding of this process should lead to a better understanding of what life is.

This belief was bolstered when scientists rediscovered Mendel's principles of genetics and when they began to assume that the genes lay somewhere in the nuclei of cells, specifically within structures called *chromosomes*. Chromosomes can be seen under the microscope, if they are properly fixed and stained with chemicals. They look much like old-fashioned sheaves of wheat, bundled and tied in the middle. During cell division the chromosomes go through a strange sort of dance. They split up and the halves migrate to opposite ends of the dividing cell, finally forming the two new nuclei of the two daughter cells formed by mitotic cell division.

Where exactly in the nuclei, however, was the genetic stuff of life? Thomas Hunt Morgan of Columbia University in New York City studied this problem in 1906, and began breeding thousands of fruit flies in order to experiment with genetic variations. Morgan selected fruit flies for his experiments because they have readily identifiable characteristics, such as eye color and wing shape, and because they reproduce rapidly and live short lives. By breeding many flies, Morgan was able to confirm the fact that genes were in some way a part of cell chromosomes.

In 1926 Hermann Joseph Muller, a member of Morgan's research team, found that he could alter the genetic characteristics of fruit flies by exposing them to X rays. The radiation caused artificial mutations of many kinds, including strange monster flies never before seen in nature. This was new proof that mutations were controlled by genes, but it did not answer the question of how.

To look at this problem, George W. Beadle and Edward L. Tatum, two other American biologists, began working in 1941 with a living system even less complicated than the fruit fly, a red bread mold, *Neurospora crassa.* The mold, which had only seven chromosomes, multiplied rapidly. It needed only sugar and a single organic material, *biotin,* for food. Tatum and Beadle exposed the mold to X rays until they created a mutation incapable of living on its normal food, biotin. When they isolated the mutation from the mold, it turned out to be an amino acid, *arginine.* Now the relationship between genes, amino acids, and protein seemed certain.

A few years later, in 1949, Linus Pauling, another American biochemist, used this knowledge to explain a complicated blood disorder, *sickle cell anemia.* A genetic disease common to black persons, sickle cell anemia results from the production of red blood cells with a characteristic sickle shape. Such cells are unable to carry normal amounts of oxygen. The disease is believed to be a genetic response among blacks to the constant threat of malaria in Africa, a response that works to their benefit in malarial areas, but that causes anemia when they live in the United States, where malaria is no longer a problem.

A British chemist, Vernon M. Ingram, then determined that hemoglobin S, the substance that causes red cells to sickle, has a slightly different arrangement of amino acids in its molecule than does normal hemoglobin, further proof that genes order the assembly of amino acids into proteins.

Chemists and biologists now knew their target—the gene itself. It was the gene that ordered the production of amino acids into proteins, which, in turn, did the work of metabolism.

But what was a gene? How was it constructed? How did it work to control the synthesis of proteins? Searching back through scientific literature, scientists rediscovered Miescher's isolation of the nucleic acid DNA. A German chemist, Robert Feulgen, then analyzed DNA from the cells of many different plants and animals and determined that it is always chemically the same, no matter where it is found.

Research on DNA and RNA went on through the 1940's. Chemists learned that the amount of DNA in a cell does not change, that the nucleus contains also RNA, and that the amount of RNA in a cell can vary. X-ray crystallographers then began studying the physical structure of the two nucleic acids. By shining weak X rays on small, purified amounts of the two substances, they obtained a kind of reflected picture, or *diffraction*, which showed bands of DNA in the chromosomes. They could not actually see the DNA itself, but they began to get an idea of what its molecular structure was like.

A few years later a British bacteriologist, Fred Griffith, made an important discovery while studying *pneumococcus*, a bacteria that causes one kind of pneumonia. Griffith was experimenting with two kinds of the same bacteria.

One was *encapsulated;* that is, covered with a thin, smooth membrane. The other form was not. Earlier research had shown that the capsule was the result of the formation of carbohydrate ordered by an enzyme.

Griffith mixed the two forms of bacteria together and injected them into a mouse. The mouse died of pneumonia. Examination of the mouse's tissues showed that it contained only a single form of pneumococcus, that with the encapsulation. Something had caused the nonencapsulated bacteria to produce a coat like that of the encapsulated form. Quickly biochemists at the Rockefeller Institute in New York City isolated and analyzed the "transforming factor" that had produced the change. They found it to be DNA. DNA clearly had the ability to create protein enzymes and to make them direct cellular reactions.

An analysis of DNA was badly needed, but its complexity made any mapping of its various parts very difficult. Chemists were able to discover that the molecule had various subgroups which, on analysis, turned out to be the now familiar adenine, guanine, cytosine, and thymine. But the puzzle of how these bases were arranged into a molecule remained. Although the molecule had to have a regular pattern, it was a complicated one, one that, for a time, could not be worked out.

A race developed in biochemical laboratories around the world to map DNA, a race that was won by an American, James Watson, and an Englishman, Francis Crick. Using X-ray diffraction pictures obtained by Maurice H. F. Wilkins and Rosalind Franklin, two other British researchers, Watson and Crick built a model of the DNA molecule—a double helix whose two strands are held together by chemical bonds between the bases.

Watson and Crick also determined that the bases bonded in pairs, and they developed the theory of DNA's replication—the splitting of the helix down its middle, its reassembly, and the role of messenger and transfer RNA in carrying messages from DNA to the ribosomes for the manufacture of protein molecules. (For a more complete description of the physical mechanics of replication and protein synthesis, see Chapter 2.)

The knowledge of how DNA is assembled and familiarity with its molecular structure offered scientists the possibility that they might be able to synthesize it in the test tube. In 1955 and 1956 biochemists made the first tentative steps in this direction. Working independently of one another, Arthur Kornberg and Severo Ochoa, two Americans, tried to replicate DNA and RNA in the laboratory. Kornberg placed a template, or sample, of DNA in a test tube and then added the elements found in DNA to the container. Ochoa performed much the same experiment with RNA. Both succeeded in making additional amounts of DNA and RNA, but their replicated samples would not make additional copies of themselves.

Several years later Kornberg managed to disassemble and put back together the DNA of a simple virus. Nevertheless, biochemists have yet to create DNA or RNA simply by mixing together the substances contained within them. Living templates of the two nucleic acids are still required to make additional copies.

The limited replication of RNA and DNA, however, suggested that it might now be possible to "read" the code contained in the arrangement of bases within these nucleic acids. Although there are only four bases in each of the two molecules, they are arranged in sequences that offer thousands of possible combinations of the four.

How many bases in combination are necessary to create a gene, the bit of information that, when translated through RNA, finally produces a collection of amino acids called a protein?

Amino Acids and Their Codons*

Amino Acid	Codons
Alanine	GCU, GCC, GCA, GCG
Arginine	CGU, CGC, CGA, CGG
	AGA, AGG
Aspartic Acid	GAU, GAC
Asparagine	AAU, AAC
Cysteine	UGU, UGC
Glutamic Acid	GAA, GAG
Glutamine	CAA, CAG
Glycine	GGU, GGC, GGA, GGG
Histidine	CAU, CAC
Isoleucine	AUU, AUC, AUA
Leucine	CUU, CUC, CUA, CUG
	UUA, UUG
Lysine	AAA, AAG
Methionine	AUG
Phenylalanine	UUU, UUC
Proline	CCU, CCC, CCA, CCG
Serine	AGU, AGC, UCU, UCC
	UCA, UCG
Threonine	ACU, ACC, ACA, ACG
Tryptophan	UGG
Tyrosine	UAU, UAC
Valine	GUU, GUC, GUA, GUG
End chain	UAA, UAG, UGA

*Adapted with permission from the 1969 *Britannica Yearbook of Science and the Future,* copyright 1969 by Encyclopaedia Britannica Inc., Chicago.

In 1961 Marshall Nirenberg, a biologist at the United States Public Health Service, attempted to answer this question. First, he obtained some tobacco mosaic virus RNA. He placed it in a sample of purified bacterial cells. The amount of protein in the sample increased to seventy-five times that of normal. The tobacco mosaic virus RNA had used elements in the bacterial cells to make protein.

Nirenberg reasoned that if this was so, it should be possible to give bacterial cells any RNA message and force them to produce protein according to the instructions in the message. If the message was known, it should be possible to predict the result. To prove this, he and an associate, Heinrich Mattahei, put together an artificial RNA composed entirely of uracil bases. They did not know which amino acid the uracil would attract, but they were almost certain it would be a single such substance. They then prepared extracts containing twenty different samples of amino acids. Each sample contained one of each of the amino acids. In each sample one of the amino acids was "tagged"—that is, a single radioactive isotope was attached to it. This made it possible to follow that amino acid through any chemical reactions that might take place. The all-uracil RNA was then added to each of the twenty extracts. In nineteen of the extracts no reaction could be followed, but in the twentieth the RNA ordered the production of a proteinlike substance composed entirely of the amino acid phenylalanine. Uracil thus seemed specific for the assembly of phenylalanine, and presumably other combinations of the four bases in RNA also were specific for the assembly of other amino acids into proteins.

This still did not tell Nirenberg and his associates the specific relationship between RNA bases and amino acids.

Many careful experiments were needed before a complete description of the "code words"—now called *codons*—and their ability to attract specific amino acids could be worked out. The relationship between codons, each consisting of three RNA bases, and amino acids is now established, however, and is described in the table on page 77.

The codon begins the amino assembly of a specific protein, but codons can also end a coding sequence and halt the production of a protein. As you can see from the table, most amino acids can be coded by more than a single codon, although in some cases there is only one codon for one amino acid, or several different codons can attract the same amino acid.

Even this knowledge, however, does not answer all the questions about replication and protein synthesis. RNA bases are undoubtedly related to DNA bases in a very specific way, but how they are related is uncertain. Equally uncertain is the number of DNA bases needed to make up a gene. Although DNA equivalents to RNA codons are probably triplets, more than one triplet may be required to create a gene.

The coding of DNA may yet be solved by the decoding of RNA. Thus it holds out the hope that man may eventually be able to understand the genetic process with enough clarity to manipulate it in response to his own desires.

Part II
Remaking Man

5

The Immortal Cell

In Phoenix, Arizona, in a cold storage vault kept at a constant 320 degrees below zero Fahrenheit, is the body of James H. Bedford, a former professor of psychology, who died at Glendale, California. Dr. Bedford's body is there because he was a member of the Life Extension Society, a group that believes it may be possible to revive the dead from the deep freeze, cure or correct the cause of their death, and restore them to life and health again.

This may seem like something from the latest science-fiction movie, but it is not without scientific foundation. Cold retards or halts the escape of water from cells, helping to prevent their death. Further, in 1972 scientists successfully froze mouse embryos and then revived them to normal life. True, the mice were healthy and normal when they were quick-frozen, and Dr. Bedford had experienced clinical death, that is, the loss of all vital signs such as breathing, heartbeat, and brain activity. Yet clinical death does not mean that all the cells of his body were dead when he was frozen; he may still, like Lazarus of the Bible, one day arise from the dead.

While many scientists and physicians doubt that such a thing is possible, others are not so sure. One of the more positive of the latter is Dr. Robert C. W. Ettinger, a professor of physics at Highland Park College in Michigan. He is the author of two books urging the freezing of human bodies for future revival and treatment, a process called *cryobiology*, a combination of the Greek words for cold and for the study of life. Dr. Ettinger and other members of the Life Extension Society believe in cryobiology so firmly that they wear identification bracelets directing that their bodies be frozen immediately after death.

One of their great hopes lies in the continuing controversy about what actually constitutes human death. Doctors once believed life ceased when the heart or the brain stopped for specific lengths of time—usually a few minutes—but recent medical research indicates that parts of the body continue to live even after this has happened. Biologists now know the sequence of events that takes place in individual cells as they die. First, all cell movement stops—if the cell is capable of independent movement. Then mitosis ceases, and DNA begins to leak out of the cell nucleus, almost as if trying to find out what is wrong. Protein synthesis then stops. After that the cell can no longer handle oxygen and lactic acid properly. The mitochondria begin to swell, and water and sodium start to invade the cell membrane. Other organelles in the cytoplasm also begin to fail.

Up to this point, cell death can be reversed by supplying the cell with the proper nutrients. Beyond this point, however, changes in the cell are irreversible, and the cell dies. All cells in an organism do not go through these steps simultaneously, so if the sequence of events can be halted by extreme cold, some cells can again be returned to life. These cells can also be removed from the organism and kept alive independently in the laboratory.

Scientists have known how to keep small groups of cells alive outside their organisms for a far longer time than the Life Extension Society has existed. Early in the twentieth century the famous scientist and Nobel Prize winner Dr. Alexis Carrel, working at the Rockefeller Institute in New York City, snipped a piece of heart muscle from the body of a living chicken and placed it in a nutrient solution in his laboratory. By feeding it the proper substances and by constantly limiting its growth, laboratory workers were able to keep this small group of cells alive for thirty-three years, two years longer than Dr. Carrel himself survived. Clearly, the death of a single organism—a single human being, for example—does not mean the immediate death of all its cells.

In another sense, all cells are immortal, anyway, because DNA, the molecule that makes them continue to live, is itself immortal. The double helix pattern of DNA ribbons back through all past living organisms to the beginning of life on this planet. So long as DNA continues to replicate in some kind of organism, life will continue in the future. Through DNA's reproduction, life, like a spark, leaps from one organism to another. Thus all organisms are merely protective containers for DNA. They exist only to shield and nourish it until the molecule can replicate and form a new organism for continued survival.

Of course, DNA does not exist by itself, and it could not continue to grow if the earth's biosphere did not provide it with a place where it could survive. DNA must have water, oxygen, nitrogen, carbon, and other elements that exist in the biosphere. In this sense, DNA is a part of the earth, and the earth is a part of life.

Yet DNA remains the only physical approach toward immortality that man knows. As its latest receptacle, he is a part of DNA's continued struggle to adapt to the earth and the biosphere. This fact has been apparent for only a short time, yet the knowledge of it has already begun to shape man's thoughts about remaking himself for continued survival. If DNA is the key molecule of living matter on earth, then all life is a continuum, and has been ever since it first evolved on earth. If this is true, one way in which man may control life is through the perpetuation of single organisms as living machines capable of being constantly repaired.

A century ago this idea would have been rejected by intelligent men. Then the death of individual human beings was accepted as inevitable, and physicians agreed that the process of individual death, once begun, was irreversible and could lead only to the failure of life. Life was not seen as a continuum, but as an interrupted series of events. Now, however, this is not so certain. More and more frequently a supposedly irreversible disease in human organisms is not seen as the end. Instead new efforts are made to maintain individual life, and the transplantation of parts from one organism into the body of another is being accepted as a way of preventing death.

Man's attempts to replace individual human tissue and organs began in the nineteenth century with blood transfusions. Blood had long been considered the most vital of body fluids. Even the ancient Greeks recognized its importance to life, but not until 1628 did the great English physician William Harvey discover the way in which the heart constantly recirculates blood through the body. Close to three more centuries were to pass before doctors attempted to transfuse it from one human being to another. Even then, most early attempts at transfusion were failures. The patient often appeared to improve after a transfusion, only to die within a few hours or days of what seemed to be some kind of poisoning. The frequent transfusion failures finally caused doctors to stop using them until early in this century a successful method of transfusion was discovered.

It was based on the work of Karl Landsteiner, an Austrian doctor who had come to the United States to work. Landsteiner found that all human blood can be divided into four general types, depending on substances called *antigens,* which are attached to the cell membrane of red cells. When antigens are introduced into a different type of blood, they cause the production of antibodies— that is, substances produced by the body to fight disease-causing organisms. These antibodies then attack the foreign antigens. Thus, as Landsteiner discovered, some types of blood will clump together, or agglutinate, if mixed with other types. This antibody-antigen reaction does not occur between all blood types, however, and transfusion is thus possible between some types, but not between others.

Landsteiner's discovery opened the way to the use of whole blood on a large scale for transfusions and the subsequent saving of thousands of lives. Because blood is both a liquid (its plasma and the chemicals dissolved in it) and made of cells (red and white cells), the transfusion of blood was the first successful transplantation of living cells from one human being to another. Blood, however, is a unique tissue. Its red cells are without nuclei and do not reproduce or make protein. Its white cells do, but they have other characteristics that make them unusual.

One of the peculiarities of red cells is that while they are incapable of making antibodies themselves, they are capable of antibody-antigen reactions. Antibodies are believed to be formed in the lymph glands, in the thymus, a gland located near the point where the neck joins the chest, and in white blood cells.

The body needs the protection of antibodies because it survives in a sea of antigens—bacteria, viruses, and other disease-causing particles or organisms. This protective barrier, the immune system, is a very individual one. Almost every human being has a set of antibodies peculiarly his own, which are able to recognize all invading antigens as foreign. A few individuals are born without any immune system at all, but they usually die at an early age because they cannot resist antigens.

Differences in immunity tend to diminish between blood relatives—brothers and sisters, parents and children —and especially between identical twins. Thought to be a product of evolution, immunity gives higher forms of life great freedom in the biosphere, because they can live side by side with microscopic organisms, as well as large ones.

In the transplantation of tissues and organs between individuals, however, or between different species, immunity can become a major problem for the success of the transplant. The very individuality of each person's own set of antibodies makes the body of the host—that is, the recipient of a transplant—attempt to destroy the organ or tissue supplied to it by a donor. The host organism either quickly or slowly—depending on a variety of circumstances—attempts to kill the transplanted foreign tissue by overwhelming it with antibodies. This causes the tissue's rejection, the loss of blood circulation and eventual death of the cells of the transplanted tissue.

The immune response was first tested experimentally

in 1923 by Dr. Emile Holman, when he was still a young surgical resident at Peter Bent Brigham Hospital in Boston. Dr. Holman attempted to graft a large number of small sections of skin—called "pinch" grafts because they were "as large as a pinch"—to the body of a badly burned five-year-old child. The skin used in the grafts was taken from the child's mother. At first the new skin appeared to "take," or grow normally, on the burned child's body, but within a few weeks the unburned areas of the child's own skin reacted with a severe rash. Only when the grafts were removed did the child recover.

From this, Dr. Holman reasoned that the large number of grafts had caused some kind of reaction in the child's immune system, although he did not know why. To test his theory, he tried a second set of grafts on a second patient. This time, however, he used three different grafts from three different donors. Much the same reaction took place. Unfortunately, although Dr. Holman later did important work in medicine at Stanford University Medical School, he did not continue his study of the rejection problem. Skin grafts between individuals were not attempted again until 1950, when two doctors at the University of California at Los Angeles, Jack Cannon and William Longmire, experimented with chickens. They succeeded in making successful skin grafts between newly hatched chickens, but when they tried to graft skin between chickens more than three days old, they had no success. By that time, the chickens had acquired enough antibodies to begin the rejection reaction.

Their work was followed by the studies of two 1960 Nobel Prize winners, Dr. Peter B. Medawar, an English physician, and Sir F. MacFarlane Burnet, an Australian. Dr. Burnet proposed a theory for the acquisition of im-

munity, and Dr. Medawar proved it in a demonstration
with mice. The Burnet theory holds that higher organisms
acquire immunity while still in their mother's womb. As
antigens circulate to the fetus from the mother's blood,
they either destroy groups, or *clones,* of cells or, in some
way, imprint on them the necessity for making antibodies.
Additional immunity, so the Burnet theory holds, is acquired after birth in much the same way, except that the
antigens now enter the body of the individual directly,
rather than from the mother.

Dr. Medawar proved Dr. Burnet's theory by injecting
skin cells from live mice into the fetuses of mice still in
the womb—hitting some and missing others—and then
placing skin grafts from the same live mice on the newly
born litter of mice after they had emerged from the
mother. The grafts on the mice that had received injected
skin cells "took," but they failed on the mice that had not
received injections. By forcing the developing immune
system of the fetal mice to recognize the injected skin
cells as their own, Dr. Medawar, had "fooled" the immune
system into accepting foreign tissue.

During the 1950's and 1960's, when these experiments
were being carried out, some progress had already been
achieved in transplanting tissue that was not served by
blood vessels from donor to host. Few tissues are not
connected to blood vessels, but one of the most important
of them is the cornea of the eye. The cornea is the clear
window through which light passes on its way to the
retina, the sensing tissue at the rear of the eyeball where
visual nerves translate light stimuli into signals for the
brain. The cornea is composed of living cells, but these
cells are not served by blood vessels. Surgeons found they
could remove corneas from the eyes of dead persons and

transplant them into the eyes of the living to replace corneal tissue that was damaged or diseased. The operation had to be performed within a few hours after the death of the donor, however. After that time, the cells in the donor tissue were no longer viable, or useful. Corneal tissue is not rejected, however, as is most blood-served tissue in the body.

Through the 1950's and 1960's eye surgeons replaced many damaged and diseased corneas. They also made a few transplants of bone, another nonblood-served portion of the body, but natural bone transplants were rapidly outmoded by artificial materials—plastics and metals, especially.

The success of eye transplants caused surgeons to look at other organs of the body with renewed interest. One of their first choices was the kidney. The kidney is affected by a number of diseases, some of which can cause sudden acute failure of this organ. Other diseases can slowly but progressively shut down its essential function, which is to cleanse the blood of the body's waste products. The kidney was selected as a candidate for transplant because it is one of several important paired organs in the body. Man normally has two kidneys, although he needs only one to survive. The extra kidney makes possible many potential donors for transplantation, because an individual can safely donate one to an individual who has lost both of his.

Both acute and progressive kidney disease can be treated temporarily by the use of artificial kidneys. The first one was constructed during World War II by a Dutch physician, Willem Kolff. Dr. Kolff, seeking ways to treat patients during the war, improvised artificial kidneys from bathtubs, sausage casing, and paddle wheels turned by an electric motor. The artificial kidneys were used to cleanse the blood of patients whose kidneys were not functioning normally until their own kidneys could take over again.

After the war more sophisticated artificial kidneys were constructed in the United States. In these kidney machines the blood was passed through sheets of plastic, and impurities were diffused through the plastic into a bath of chemicals. The new artificial kidneys were greatly assisted by the addition of a plastic *shunt*, or pipe, in the patient's arm or leg, which connected an artery to the machine. Kidney patients could plug into the machine for several hours each week and use its action to replace the function of their natural kidneys. Such *dialysis* did not replace the diseased or injured kidney itself, but it did offer longer life to kidney patients.

In the meantime research into kidney transplantation had begun. The first transplantation of human kidneys was made by Dr. James V. Scola at Springfield Hospital, Boston, in March 1951. The transplant was rejected within a few days, however. Two years later, in 1953, Dr. David M. Hume, a surgeon at Peter Bent Brigham Hospital in Boston, performed a second kidney transplant. His patient survived for 175 days before rejection took place. A series of subsequent kidney transplants, however, were far less successful, and Dr. Hume eventually abandoned his work and left the hospital. Transplantation then was taken over by Dr. Joseph Murray. By using a number of special drugs that interfere with protein synthesis—and hence with the production of antibodies—Dr. Murray gradually lengthened the time before transplanted kidneys were rejected from days to months and then to years.

Dr. Murray used another method as well to forestall the

work of antibodies—he transplanted kidneys between identical twins. The similarity of antibodies in such individuals helped to reduce rejection, and several twins lived for long periods with transplanted kidneys. Few kidney-disease victims, however, are fortunate enough to have healthy identical twins. As a result, transplant surgeons began to seek other sources of donor kidneys, first blood relatives and then persons who had been dead only minutes or hours. By the careful use of drugs, a longer time elapsed before rejection occurred, and today both kidney transplantation and artificial kidneys are used in the treatment of kidney disease.

The success of kidney and eye transplants now led doctors to consider other organs of the body for spare-parts surgery. One of the most tempting was the heart. The heart is not a paired organ and, because it is not, donor hearts can come only from the body of someone who has just died. In addition, removal of a diseased heart means almost certain death for the patient who rejects a transplant, in contrast to a return to an artificial kidney for a patient whose kidney transplant fails.

Work on heart transplants also began in the 1950's at Stanford University Medical School in California. There a young assistant professor of surgery, Dr. Norman Shumway, was able to transplant the heart of one dog into the body of another, which lived for as long as a year. Dr. Shumway used a technique that removed much of the diseased muscle, but left most of the major blood vessels to the heart intact. He was contemplating a similar operation on a human being in 1967, but a few weeks before he planned to attempt it, Dr. Christiaan Barnard of South Africa performed the first heart transplant on a grocer suffering from advanced heart disease. The replacement heart came from a young woman who had been fatally injured in an automobile accident.

The patient died of pneumonia eighteen days later, but Dr. Barnard's example was followed by other surgeons around the world. Several hundred heart transplants were performed with great public interest and attention. Most of the recipients lived only a short time after their operations, however. Their bodies quickly rejected the transplanted tissue. The problem of overcoming the immune reaction of the body remained to be solved, and within a year, most surgeons had stopped transplantation of the heart. Only Dr. Shumway continued his work, with increasing success.

The wide publicity given heart transplants, however, did have the beneficial effect of creating public interest in the possibility of transplants and in the need for donated tissues and organs. Surgeons experimentally transplanted the lungs, the liver, the pancreas, the ovaries, the heart valves, the middle bones of the ear, skin, bone marrow, and bone in general. Gradual progress was made in overcoming rejection of tissues, and human transplantation became at least an accepted experimental way of treating disease when no other alternative remained.

Physicians also began to explore the use of artificial organs. Man-made replacements for parts of the human body are hardly new. Wooden legs, crutches, and canes have served as substitutes for limbs lost through injury or disease for centuries. Even spectacles and false teeth are not new. Most such efforts at artificial replacement of natural organs, however, were until recently concerned with the exterior of the body. Not until the invention of tough, durable, light plastics, which could not be broken down by body chemicals, did the possibility of placing artificial devices inside the body become a reality. Dacron, nylon, silicone rubber, and similar substances made the fashioning of substitute blood vessels a way of correcting some arterial diseases. In the 1950's surgeons began re-placing sections of the *aorta*, the largest blood vessel in the body, with dacron and nylon substitutes. The aorta, in particular, is often damaged by the formation of an *aneurysm*, a swelling and ballooning of the blood-vessel wall, caused by a weakening of its lining. In other cases, the aorta may be narrowed by the formation of deposits of cholesterol, a biochemical carried in the blood that forms bumps and obstructions called *plaques* inside the blood vessel. Surgeons removed these damaged sections of aorta and sewed substitute vessels made of plastic in their place. After a few months the interior of the artificial vessel was covered with a natural lining and blood flowed through the new artery section without difficulty.

Plastic implants have been used also to repair vocal cords and for the plastic surgical reconstruction of parts of the body lost because of injury or disease. They have even been used to increase the breast measurements of topless dancers.

The ear, too, has benefited from plastic replacement of some of its parts. Sound is conducted to the brain by the eardrum, by three small bones of the middle ear— the *malleus, incus,* and *stapes*—and by the inner ear. In certain infections the middle ear bones may be lost. Plastic replacements can be built for them to help restore hearing. A more satisfactory method of correction, how-ever, is the removal of the three bones from a dead person and their transplantation into the ear of a living person. By fashioning an eardrum from a section of vein and attaching it to the transplanted middle ear bones, doctors, have almost completely restored the hearing of some persons. The success of the surgery depends on the patient's having a good inner ear and auditory nerve, however.

Their growing success with plastic devices and replacements led surgeons to construct such *prostheses* for the heart. Silicone rubber was the first material used to make replacements for heart valves, often damaged by disease. It, however, proved unsatisfactory. Dr. Charles A. Hufnagel, an American surgeon, then developed a valve based on the movement of a plastic ball inside a stainless-steel cage. As the blood moves through the heart, it forces the ball upward, opening the valve. The force of gravity causes the ball to drop back into the valve seat and close the valve when the heart is not pumping.

Surgeons and electronic engineers have also been able to construct artificial *pacemakers.* Normally, the heart's beat is regulated by a small group of cells at its right side, which send bursts of electrical energy into the heart's muscle, causing it to contract. When this natural pacemaker fails, it is possible to replace its electrical stimulation with a tiny electric battery and timer. The first artificial pacemakers were connected to the heart by a stainless-steel wire protruding through the skin to a battery worn outside the body. Newer models have tiny nuclear-powered batteries, which are surgically implanted inside the body. They must be replaced every four or five years because the battery wears out.

Neither pacemaker nor heart-valve operations would be possible were it not for the invention of the heart-lung machine, a device that takes over the normal action of the heart and lungs during surgery. The first successful heart-lung device was built in the 1930's in the United States by Dr. Alexis Carrel and the famous American aviator Charles A. Lindbergh, but it was used only on experimental animals.

The first such machine to be used on humans was perfected by Dr. John Gibbon and used by him at the Mayo Clinic in 1952. It consists of a large plastic bag, two plastic tubes or *catheters*, and a small electrically operated pump. The catheters are inserted into a vein and an artery —usually one of the two *venae cavae*, the major veins leading into the heart, and the *femoral artery* in the leg. Blood is drawn from the vein, trickles down through the plastic bag, where it is bubbled with oxygen, and is then pumped back into the body through the artery. While the machine is operating, it both pumps the blood and oxygenates it, leaving the surgeon free to operate directly on the heart itself. In theory, the heart-lung machine could serve as an artificial heart indefinitely, much as does the artificial kidney. In practice, however, use of the machine is limited to a few hours because of the damage it does to red blood cells. But the existence of the machine suggests that an artificial heart could be built, some kind of small pump that could be permanently installed in the body to replace a natural heart unable to work as it should.

Several partial artificial hearts have been used to replace the action of the ventricles, the two lower chambers of the heart, which are the source of the chief pumping action of its muscle. Attempts to build a complete artificial replacement for the heart have been less successful for two reasons: damage to red blood cells and problems in supplying power to such an artificial pump. Neither of these two obstacles seems impossible to overcome, however, and artificial hearts may one day be as available as are artificial kidneys.

Thus the development of artificial internal and external replacements for human parts raises the possibility of a semiartificial man whose life may be prolonged by a combination of transplanted and man-made organs and tissues. Even so delicate a tissue as the blood may one day be replaced by the proper mixture of its vital chemicals.

It is possible to imagine a man who is completely artificial, as well. Some scientists have dubbed this creation a *cyborg*, a term originally used in science fiction. In the sense that many people are living today because they have transplanted or artificial organs of one kind or another, man already has achieved a partially artificial being. A complete cyborg, however, probably lies some distance in the future. Such a creature would be assembled of atoms and molecules artificially put together by other men, and he would be exactly like his human counterpart. If this is possible, each human being might well have his own matching cyborg. Then, if he suffered injury or disease, the appropriate part could be removed from his cyborg and transplanted into him. Similarly, if human-like cyborgs could be created, it should also be possible to assemble humanoids that are similar to man but do not have some of his handicaps. Cyborgs capable of living under water like fish might be constructed. Others might be made to live in space with minimal supplies of oxygen. Cyborgs would be easy to repair, have a longer life, and possess an untiring ability to work, as well as having other advantages. What their thinking processes might be is uncertain. A nightmare often raised in science fiction is a world where cyborgs or some other nearly human artificial creatures succeed man as the ultimate product of evolution—a creature that is a combination of machine and life itself, but without the ability to reason. Just as robots are equipped to do a single task endlessly and unfailingly, cyborgs might perform tasks for which humans would no longer be needed.

Some parts of this nightmare already exist. Men and machines are already parts of complex systems. The modern jet aircraft has a pilot, but he is largely a minor decision maker in a complicated system that includes not only his brain and body, but ground radar, air-traffic controllers, radio signals, automatic pilots, and delicate instruments that fly the plane "blind" in bad weather. A jet plane is seldom dependent solely on what the pilot can see, touch, and hear himself.

Man has come to rely on many such combinations of human and machine decision making today: automatic elevators, heart monitors in hospitals, air conditioning and heating thermostats, a whole host of devices that, once set in action, work by themselves within the limits for which they have been programmed. Man may one day become an even more intimate part of such systems. Perhaps one day he may plug directly into small computers to expand his reasoning and calculating capacity without the present, often cumbersome, methods of entering and removing information from machines.

In the meantime, man also seems likely to require more and more replacement parts from the bodies of the dead to sustain the living. Today he stands on the threshold of general spare-parts surgery and human transplantation, dependent only on his ability to overcome the immune response and on his learning how to collect and bank living tissues and organs. The practical limit to human transplantation is neither the techniques of surgery nor the long survival of donor materials after death. Rather, it is in finding ways to gather such materials in an organized fashion. Individuals may not be immortal, but their cells may well enjoy far longer lives than they have in the past. The future of man seems to lie in his ability to adapt machines to his use and to combine them with natural organs for longer individual existence.

6

Engineering the Gene

In 1932 the English novelist Aldous Huxley published a now famous novel, *Brave New World*. Its opening scenes depict a time in the future when babies are artificially conceived in the laboratory by mixing egg and sperm cells and then grown in glass-bottle "wombs" before being "decanted" instead of being born. At the time the book was published, few of its predictions, including artificial conception and birth, were expected to become reality, but by the 1960's at least four medical research workers, Dr. Daniele Petrucci of Italy and Drs. John Rock, Landrum B. Settles, and Cecil Jacobson of the United States had succeeded in fertilizing human egg cells with human sperm in the laboratory. The cells they created lived only a few days, but they proved that artificial conception and controlled birth may become a fact before this century is over.

Man's physical control and modification of himself today includes vaccination and transplantation, but he may soon extend his domination of life to the time before birth. Some of the reasons for seeking to do so are clear. If man can control the formation of himself by making human bodies from their beginning, he may also control the *way* in which they are made by selecting the genes in the nuclei of his sperm and egg cells. He may then be able to eliminate many, perhaps all, of the random combinations of genes which produce the defects that today are a part of natural birth. Today everyone has individual peculiarities that set him apart from others. Identical twins come closest to being genetically the same, but most people have some differences or variations from the norm. There is no typical human being.

The most obvious defects that occur because of defective genes are mental retardation, missing hands, arms, legs, or feet, improperly formed spines, or cleft palates. Although these things are obvious, they are not the most common genetic defects. Millions of human beings are born with myopic vision, slightly clubbed feet, major or minor birthmarks, or allergies to many different substances. Such variations are taken for granted today as the random combination of genes obtained by a new individual from his mother and father.

In *Brave New World,* few of these defects exist. Huxley's future is a time when it is possible to select only the best or most wanted genes through the total control of reproduction. In *Brave New World* sexual reproduction is forbidden—indeed, motherhood is considered a perversion —and sex is used only for pleasure. The decision as to which genes are to be permitted to continue is decided by "controllers," master genetic planners, who agree on how many and what kind of people should be turned out by the world's biological assembly lines. Huxley predicted that laboratory reproduction would permit the selection of specific types, a few of them highly intelligent "Alphas," intended to be future controllers, the rest a series of graded castes, each created for a special task in the world.

While controlled human reproduction remains to be achieved, it is already a reality in the breeding of plants and animals. Man, as a supercontroller for other species, now creates special kinds of plants and animals for special reasons. By using selected cereal grains, he seeks to produce the special kinds of wheat, corn, and rice of the "Green Revolution," which has doubled and tripled cereal grain production in Mexico, India, Pakistan, Japan, and the Philippines, and made even greater crop gains possible in the United States and Europe.

Plant breeders work with banks of seeds with known genetic characteristics. Using the principles established by Mendel in his pea-planting experiments, plant scientists have been able to grow wheat that will not "lodge," or fall over in wet soil, which has large, many-kerneled heads, and is highly resistant to plant pests and diseases. By picking strains of grain with the desired characteristics and breeding them through many generations, scientists can create plants never before seen in nature.

Man could do the same thing with himself now, if he were willing to allow his reproductive processes to be placed under strict controls. *Eugenics,* as this is sometimes called, could be accomplished today, if man were willing to limit sexual reproduction to carefully selected partners. The idea is not unthinkable, but it is prohibited by present-day ideas of personal human freedom. Even so, such control is already practiced in genetic counseling. Potential parents who know they carry genes that could cause their children to be born with defects can go to genetic counselors for information about the dangers (or lack of them) in conceiving such children. The decision as to whether to have a child remains with the parents, but often they decide not to risk having defective children after counseling. Thus they have engaged in selective and voluntary eugenics.

No such restraints on cooperation exist in the breeding of domestic livestock and pets. Controlled reproduction is a part of raising livestock throughout most of the world. Breeders usually seek stock with the best gene characteristics for good meat production. Many animals, however, never see their mates. It is estimated, for example, that fifty million cattle are born in the United States each year from a combination of *sperm banking* and *superovulation*. Bull sperm is taken from prize bulls and quick-frozen. In superovulation cows are fed female hormones, which force them to produce many more egg cells than they will need. Some of the eggs are removed and implanted in nonpregnant cows. The egg cells are then fertilized by *artificial insemination* with the bull sperm after it has been properly thawed.

Scientists at the laboratories of Schering Company in Berlin, Germany, also have had some experimental success in artificially increasing the number of male offspring by screening semen. Male-producing sperm in the semen have a tendency to move more rapidly than those that will produce females. By separating the faster "swimmers" from slower-moving sperm, and by artificially inseminating females, the chances of the conception of males have been increased, Schering workers have reported in *Nature*, a British scientific journal.

In the same journal two American scientists, Dorothea Bennett of Cornell University Medical College, and Edward A. Boyse of Memorial Sloan-Kettering Cancer Center, report they have been able to increase slightly the chances of female births in mice through immunological treatment, in effect killing sperm that might create males.

For the present, neither of the two methods seems likely to be used without artificial insemination, which makes them of limited value in human conception. They may be of value in the control of livestock reproduction, however.

Still another technique used in livestock production that could be applied to human reproduction is the use of *surrogate mothers*. In 1961 a shipment of female rabbits was flown from South Africa to England. Each rabbit contained the embryo* of a healthy sheep, taken from its natural mother and carefully inserted in the rabbit's womb. The rabbits served only as smaller carrying cases during air shipment. In England the sheep embryos were removed from the rabbits and reimplanted in female sheep. Later they were born naturally and grew into healthy animals. Much the same technique has been used by Israel to import cattle.

Superovulation, artificial insemination, and the use of surrogate mothers are only three new methods of reproduction. It is also possible now to fuse several different cells in the test tube to make one, which then grows into a healthy animal. Mouse cells have been combined in this way.

Experiments are being made as well in reproduction by *vegetative multiplication*. Plant breeders and gardeners have known for a long time that it is possible to cut a branch from a plant or flower, place it in the ground, and have a new plant grow from the cutting. Genetically,

---

*Technically, a mammal is called an embryo during the first two months of development in its mother's womb. Thereafter, it is called a fetus until it is born.

the new plant is exactly like the one from which it was taken. The same process is now being attempted in animal cells. Nuclei have been removed from frog cells and new nuclei have been added, in an attempt to form a line of identical animal cells. The technique is known as *cloning*. Such experiments have been partly successful in frogs. Frog cells, however, are much larger than animal reproductive cells, particularly sperm, and the methods of doing such experiments in mammals have yet to be worked out.

At the United States Agricultural Experimental Station at Beltsville, Maryland, there is a strain of turkeys that seems to be producing by *asexual* means; that is, the turkey hens continue to lay fertile eggs from generation to generation, even though the strain has not been fertilized by cocks. Why the eggs are fertile is still a mystery, but it may be because of a virus. In that case, it may be possible to control the asexual conception of a species, perhaps even man, in the future.

In fact, all these biological techniques may well be applicable to human reproduction. If superovulation is possible in cattle, it could also be achieved in humans. It has, in fact, already happened accidentally. Women who have difficulty in becoming pregnant have been given special drugs to regulate their ovulation. In a few instances the drugs have caused the birth of twins, triplets, quadruplets, quintuplets, and even sextuplets.

The use of frozen sperm in human beings is a reality, too. Men undergoing *vasectomies* to make them sterile— that is, the surgical closing of the tubes that lead from the testicles to the penis—can first have their sperm quick-frozen and stored in sperm banks for possible future use. Then if, at some time in the future, they decide they wish to father children, the sperm can be thawed and artificially inseminated in their wives. In fact, some women have already undergone artificial insemination. Women who wish to have children, but who are unable to conceive because their husbands produce nonviable, or nonfertile, sperm, today can obtain sperm from men they will never meet. While artificial insemination is not a common practice, it is being carried out in the United States and other countries. Sperm is obtained from paid volunteers, quick-frozen, then thawed and artificially introduced into the waiting mother-to-be.

Thus the combination of superovulation and artificial insemination predicted in *Brave New World* could happen. Volunteer women might someday agree to become superovulating "factories" for the production of human egg cells. Their cells could then be "harvested" and implanted in women willing, but unable, to conceive children. The egg cells could then be artificially inseminated with viable sperm from male volunteers, who would never see either the women who produced the egg cells or the women in which fertilization would take place. Beyond this, it is only a step or two to the elimination of natural mothers completely and their replacement with the glass-jar wombs in the laboratories of *Brave New World*.

Children born by artificial conception, however, would still carry the genes given them by their mothers and fathers. Beyond artificial conception, therefore, lies gene control, the ability to regulate the matching of genes for the mass production of human beings—the ultimate prediction of *Brave New World*.

The control of genes, however, is not as simple as the control of reproduction. Although man now understands with some clarity what a gene is—a portion of the sequence of the DNA molecule—he remains unsure of the length of such sequences and their location in the double helix of the molecule. Moreover, the way in which genes control the growth of cells and their reproduction is not understood very well either. Most genes seem to do their work through the regulation of protein synthesis, especially those proteins that are enzymes.

Genes also seem to be capable of starting and stopping protein synthesis at proper times in the life of the cell and, by so doing, controlling cell differentiation and cell growth. But how? One theory is that some of them are operator genes. Built into them in some way are methods of creating enzymes at just the right time. Some of these enzymes also seem to be capable of starting and stopping other genes. For example, as an embryo or fetus grows, it reaches various stages of development when cell multiplication must stop. The orders for such a shutdown in protein synthesis must be contained in the original DNA brought together when the egg was fertilized. But how this information is coded into the DNA and how it is expressed or transmitted is still not known. Jacques Monod, a French biologist, has discovered and identified operator genes—genes that control other genes—in bacteria, but if such master controls exist in human cells, they have yet to be found. Almost certainly, however, they must exist.

Several medical research scientists have suggested that a similar process may be at work in reverse in the development of cancer cells. Instead of DNA's regulating protein synthesis through messages to RNA, these scientists say, RNA may be giving orders to DNA, unlocking locked or repressed genes, and sending protein synthesis off on irregular paths. This possible reverse transcription may even alter DNA itself. If this is what really happens, it may provide a partial answer to the mystery of cancer, one of man's least understood diseases. Cancer is a wild and often erratic growth of cells that exist at the expense of the organism in which they live. If there is such a process as reverse transcription, perhaps it is set in operation by a sudden backward switch in biological gears within the cell. What might make such an event take place? Some scientists believe it may be the result of a wandering wild virus that has entered the cell.

Viruses are peculiar objects that exist at the edge of life. They seem to be neither completely alive nor completely inert. Most of them have a core of DNA surrounded by a coating of protein. A few, however, have a core of RNA. Viruses do not live except as parasites. They have neither cytoplasm nor cytoplasmic organelles. Outside the cell, they are inert. Inside it, they flourish, using material stolen from the cell to reproduce themselves.

Viruses have an uncertain place in the evolutionary development of life. They may be semiorganisms that never developed an independent existence, or they may be the first primitive steps life made before cells came into being. Whatever their history, they are objects of great interest to biochemical researchers, who have been able to take them apart and put them back together again, something that has yet to be accomplished with more complicated cells.

The ability of viruses to invade cells and steal their protoplasm was discovered in the 1950's by several biologists working with a particular kind of such semilife, called *phages*. Phages are larger than many viruses. One of the most studied phage viruses is the T2 virus, a peculiar mallet-shaped object with a head, a tail, or "handle," and spidery-shaped "legs," which allow the virus particle to settle on the surface of a cell. There the T2 phage pierces the cell wall and injects its DNA—coiled inside its head —into the cell's cytoplasm. Inside the cell the phage DNA quickly acquires the necessary materials for reproduction and begins to forge copies of itself. In time, the rapidly multiplying new phage particles take over the cell, break its membrane, and stream out to other nearby cells to reproduce themselves again. Simpler viruses probably do much the same thing, except that they are able to slip through the cell membrane whole.

Despite their minute size—some are so small they can barely be seen even under the great magnification of the electron microscope—viruses do have genes. They are far fewer in number than those in human cells, a fact that makes them important in the study of gene character- istics and gene defects.

Defects in gene construction—actually defects in the arrangement of DNA sequences—seem to fall into two general categories. The first group is the result of the improper assembly of DNA at the time of the union of cells in sexual reproduction. Improper formation of genes can cause serious defects in humans. *Mongolism,* or *Down's syndrome,* a form of mental retardation, is an example. This disorder is caused by the improper separa- tion of chromosomes, and Mongols have forty-seven in- stead of the normal forty-six chromosomes. Mongoloid children have peculiar rounded faces with vaguely orien- tal features. They can learn little and usually live only for a short time. The defect cannot be corrected by any known method of medical treatment.

A second large group of birth defects, however, may lend itself to gene control. These disorders are caused by genes that order improper, unnecessary, or insufficient protein synthesis—a fact that gives this group of defects another name, inborn errors of metabolism.

Phenylketonuria (PKU) is an inborn error of metabolism that results from an inability to convert *phenylalanine,* an amino acid, into tyrosine in the liver. The inability to carry out this normal function of metabolism apparently happens because a gene either orders too much or not enough of an as-yet-unidentified enzyme. As a result, too much phenylalanine accumulates in the body. In time this can lead to mental retardation. The disorder can be detected by a simple blood test—now required in many states of the United States—and the effects of the disease can be averted by feeding such children a diet free of phenylalanine.

Unfortunately, not all inborn errors of metabolism can be treated by diet. It would be far more satisfactory if man could, in some way, reconstruct or alter genes in a defective fetus before it is born. By removing small samples of *amniotic fluid,* the fluid surrounding an unborn child in its mother's womb, scientists can now test cells for such defects. Although scientists do not yet know how to alter or reconstruct genes, they have suggested several possible ways by which they could. One would be to force cells to accept correct DNA segments for those that are coded with the wrong kind of information. To accomplish this, of course, they would first have to find the proper place in the DNA helix for gene substitution to take place. Second, they would have to remove a correct DNA sequence from other cells. Third, the correct DNA message would have to be introduced into the cell and used to replace the "bad" DNA fragment.

The task would be difficult because DNA is a fragile

molecule that breaks down easily under chemical stress. If scientists are to carry out gene correction, DNA must somehow be protected against such damage during its passage into the cell. Despite the difficulties involved, biologists have already made some tentative steps toward gene transplantation.

In 1969 scientists at the Department of Microbacteriology at Harvard University Medical School isolated a pure gene from a bacterial cell. A few months later in 1970 another group at the Institute for Enzyme Research at the University of Wisconsin made a synthetic gene for a yeast cell. Both groups pointed out that many other steps still remain before either of these experiments will lead to genetic transplantation. Both agreed, however, that this kind of surgery is possible.

Such an operation has been outlined by two other scientists, Theodore Friedmann of the Salk Institute in San Diego, California, and Richard Roblin of the Infectious Disease Unit at Massachusetts General Hospital in Boston. Writing in *Science* magazine, the two predict that DNA sections can be inserted into the cell in one of two ways.

First, the DNA in human cells might be isolated and the necessary fragment or fragments extracted and purified. Then this minute portion of foreign DNA might be forced into the defective cell by *phagocytosis*, the same process by which white blood cells engulf and digest antigens in the bloodstream.

An alternative suggestion is the insertion of the DNA segment into the cell by making it a part of a small virus, either real or synthetic. Because viruses have little difficulty in penetrating the cell wall, the necessary DNA segment might, in a way not yet discovered, be hooked to the virus before it passed into the cell. After entering the cell, the virus might—again in a way as yet unknown —be made to surrender the DNA fragment for incorporation into the proper place in the cell's DNA.

This model system, of course, leaves many unanswered questions. How, for example, is the virus to be made to give up its DNA "cargo"? How can the virus or DNA fragment be directed to the proper cell? Once inside the cell, what will send the DNA fragment to the cell's DNA and what will cause it to replace the unwanted DNA fragment there? How can the unwanted DNA then be removed from the cell?

Drs. Friedmann and Roblin also point out three other problems. First, not enough is yet known about how genes regulate the production of enzymes to be sure simply replacing one bit of DNA with another would correct the cell's faulty machinery. Second, DNA fragments, even those that are "good" for the cell, might, like transplanted tissue and organs, be seen by the cell as foreign and thus be rejected by it. Third, and perhaps most important, if genetic mechanics and repair are made possible, who is to decide which genes should be used, how they are to be used, and on whom treatment is to be carried out?

This last problem has been posed in many different ways by many biologists and nonscientists. Who is to decide who the controllers envisioned in Huxley's *Brave New World* are to be? They will have the power of life and death over many other persons. Few would disagree with the aims of genetic engineering, the control and elimination of such diseases as Mongolism and PKU. In striving toward this goal, however, man must also learn to control the action of all genes. He will then have effective control over the evolution of life itself. Even as he now controls the evolution of some animals and plants, someday he may rule all living organisms. Who is to decide how he is to use this power? In tampering with natural selection, may he not also be committing biological suicide?

The study of evolution shows, at least to many biologists, that man has evolved because he is the best present answer to the conditions under which life must exist on earth. This may not mean, however, that he is the final answer. By halting any further random combination of genes, by halting any hope of adaptation to a changing earth, he may eventually find it impossible to change as the planet changes.

One of the best summaries of man's concerns in genetic engineering has been written by two nonscientists, Senator John V. Tunney of California and his administrative assistant, Meldon E. Levine. They pose ten questions they believe must be answered before a program of engineering human genes can be put into effect:

1. Which characteristics are most desirable and who is to decide which they are?

2. Will the control of genes make all men the same, and, if it does, is this desirable?

3. When should genetic control take place: in the unfertilized egg, in the sperm, in the embryo, in the fetus, in infancy, in adulthood? Who is to decide when?

4. What is the difference between curing genetic defects and controlling all genes, including those of "normal" men?

5. Are genetic controls to be limited to only a single human being at one time or are they to be expanded to large masses of persons?

6. What is a "normal" human being? Who is to decide what is "normal" in human development?

7. After normality has been defined—if such a definition can be reached—how can this definition be applied to genetic engineering?

8. Will genetic engineering make children superior to their parents, and if this should happen, what effect will it have on the already widening gap between the generations?

9. What effect would genetic engineering have on man's individual worth and dignity? Will men be graded genetically into the castes or levels foreseen in *Brave New World?*

10. Once genetic engineering has been achieved, who is to decide who will receive it and who will not?

This final question contains the dilemma that man faces in all his efforts to modify and control himself. Does any man have the right to control the physical being of another? Can man really control nature? Can one man or a single group of men finally achieve control over the life and death of others?

Since civilization began man has, on frequent occasions, surrendered his life to others. Since the founding of Sumer over five thousand years ago, soldiers have placed their lives in the hands of their commanders. Since the beginning of medical treatment, every patient, by agreeing to obey his physician, has given to him the power of life and death. Yet not until the past two hundred years has this surrender of self also involved the use of machines controlled either by strangers or by devices that, once set in motion, are operated by no one.

The use of an artificial kidney can prolong the life of

a patient with chronic kidney disease today, but there are many more chronic kidney patients than there are kidney machines. Persons other than the kidney patient must decide who among the many in need of the machines can be allowed to use them. Once that decision has been made, whether it is right or wrong, it is the machine, not a human being, that preserves human life.

In the same way, genetic engineering may come to save lives or prevent disabling illness. Yet it may not be possible to save every human being who could benefit by the control of the genes. "Controllers" of some kind must decide how genetics is to be applied to those suffering from inborn errors of metabolism. Who is to name the controllers of genetic engineering? Does man really know enough to make such a choice wisely? His history offers no assurance that he does. Neither does it offer any assurance that he may not someday be able to do so.

7

The Flame of Life

Strike a match, then blow it out. This act is at once one
of the simplest and most profound symbols of man's
evolution. It represents both one of man's greatest discoveries and one of his most serious problems in survival.
Symbolized in the lighting and extinguishing of a match
is man's ability to start, stop, and control fire and to use
the energy its flame produces. Without fire in its many
forms, man might still be only a step or two removed
from other animals. They fear fire; he respects it. They
flee it; he seeks to control and use its power.

The discovery of fire predates man's recorded history.
No one knows when the first human being knowingly
struck a flame, watched it burn, and then put it out, just
as the precise dates when man acquired language and
learned to use the wheel are uncertain. With the discovery
of fire, however, man gradually came to understand that
it would give him heat and light, temper metal, cook
food, and help him with a host of other tasks, including,
in a later era, the steady production of energy to operate
machines.

Probably the first man-made fire was an accident, perhaps caused by a spark struck from rocks into dry tinder,
perhaps by the rapid rotation of one stick against another,
two of the ways in which some of the world's primitive

peoples still make fire without matches. Certainly man had also seen fire before he learned to use it. Perhaps he saw lightning strike into trees or grassland and set them aflame. His great discovery was that he could both create and control fire as he wished. As soon as he was able to do that, he also found that his flame had to be constantly fed with fuel or it would go out.

Man did not know it then, but he was to learn that fire is probably unique to the planet earth. Fire is the reaction of free oxygen in the atmosphere—that is, oxygen not combined with other elements—with combustible substances, or fuels, found on or in the earth's crust. Except for Mars, no other planet in the solar system has sufficient free oxygen in its atmosphere to permit burning. The lack of oxygen on other planets also makes it unlikely that they are able to support life, at least life as it is found on earth.

Today we tend to take the fact of earthly fire for granted and to assume that our planet has an unlimited supply of substances that can be used for fuel. Unfortunately, this is not true. Combustion is limited to those materials that will oxidize readily and rapidly in the atmosphere—coal, wood, oil, oil shale, and natural gas. All of these materials are rich in carbon and, except for wood, come from deposits, probably of plant and animal materials, laid down in the earth's rocks eons ago. Because the substances apparently were formed from the compression of once living materials under intense heat and pressure, they are often referred to as fossil fuels. Fossil fuels burn readily in the atmosphere and, in variously refined forms, are most familiar to us as gasoline, kerosine, propane, butane, and other fractions or parts of petroleum.

Such fuels are irreplaceable. Once burned, their energy cannot be reused.

To illustrate this problem—central to understanding man's present crisis in energy—strike another match and do not blow it out. The match soon disappears into smoke, ashes, and a stub of carbonized wood. Without thinking about it, we "know" the match cannot again be used to make heat and light. Its mass of material has been dispersed by fire. Without infinite care, and probably not even then, its individual atoms cannot be rejoined into the molecules that would again make it a match. Once destroyed, it can never be put back together again. Yet why? All that the match was, still exists somewhere in the universe. Why then can it not be used again?

Nineteenth-century physicists and chemists puzzled over this problem for many years before they reached a reasonable solution to the paradox. From many experiments they discovered the laws of *thermodynamics*—a combination of Greek words meaning movement of heat. The first law of thermodynamics is that energy can be changed from one form to another, but it cannot be created or destroyed. One form of energy is heat, and scientists noticed that in any reaction in which heat is freed from matter, the heat always moves from the hottest place in the system toward the coolest. To illustrate this, imagine two vessels, both containing water and air and connected to one another by a closed passage. If one of the vessels is heated but the other is not, the water in the heated vessel will eventually turn to steam and move through the passage between the two to the cooler vessel.

There the steam will meet the cooler water of the second vessel and condense into water again. Eventually, the heat will be exhausted from the cooler water in the second vessel to the air around it. Thereafter it will be dispersed into the atmosphere. Once it has passed from the second vessel into the atmosphere, it cannot be recovered and reused again as long as the temperatures remain the same. The water in the second vessel cannot be turned into steam and forced back into the first vessel unless it is heated to a temperature higher than that of the first vessel. It is possible to create an equilibrium between the two vessels by maintaining the same temperature in the water in both of them, but it is impossible to reverse the flow of heat from the second (cooler) vessel to the first (warmer) one.

From such experiments, physicists have concluded that energy, once liberated from matter, flows only in one direction, away from the hottest point toward the coolest. This is the second law of thermodynamics. The third law follows from it. If all energy flows only in one direction, away from its point of liberation, then all energy liberated from matter becomes more and more disassociated from itself. This quality is called *entropy*, and it helps to explain why energy cannot be recaptured for reuse once it has been expended in an energetic reaction. Just as we cannot put a match back together again to be struck and relighted, neither can we reclaim the energy liberated from a gallon of gasoline or a lump of coal, once it has been burned, or freed. Even though the energy involved in the reaction has not been destroyed, it has been so dispersed that it is no longer useful.

The second and third laws of thermodynamics are important because they help explain man's growing crisis in energy. Man's energy requirements today are far greater than they were early in his history. All he needed then was wood to burn for fire and warmth. Only gradually did he come to understand that coal and oil could be burned for the same purposes—heat and light. Not until the past hundred years of his time on earth has he learned to refine petroleum into gasoline and other usable fractions for powering machines. The discovery of fuels and of machines capable of using them is one of the two events that have greatly accelerated man's need for energy. The second has been a constantly increasing population.

Homo sapiens has been on the earth for at least fifty thousand years, probably longer, but most of this time his numbers have been small. The first great increase in the world's human population came after the end of the Ice Ages as man settled into cities, towns, and villages. The earth then probably was home to only about ten million persons. By the time of Christ, almost two thousand years ago, this figure had risen to 250 million. In 1650 it stood at half a billion. Today the earth's population is at least three and a half billion, perhaps almost four billion. If these figures are plotted on a graph, they make a curve that is almost flat for hundreds of years and then suddenly climbs almost vertically during the past few centuries.

An increase in human numbers alone would be enough for more energy to be required from the earth, but the sudden increase in men in the world has also been accompanied by a growing reliance on machines to do man's work. This has placed an added burden on the earth's fuel reserves. Until the Industrial Revolution man mostly did his work by expending his own personal energy. His tools were hoes, rakes, shovels, axes, and hammers, all physical extensions of his hands or feet. As the plow and wheeled vehicles were invented, man turned to domesticated draft animals for more energy. Still later he learned to use the power of moving water and wind. However, not until he was able to invent true engines, machines that work by burning fuel, could he effectively use the earth's fuel resources. The machines man came to invent did vastly more work than he could do by hand, but they also required much greater amounts of fuel.

Since then, as man's desire for machines has increased, so has his demand for energy. He has searched over the crust of the earth for hidden pools of oil, ripped up its surface to mine for coal, tapped pockets of natural gas, and built tankers, pipelines, refineries, power plants, electrical transmission systems, and dams—and yet his demand for energy grows ever greater. Only recently has he come to understand that the earth's supplies of fossil fuels are limited and rapidly running out. The United States, the largest single user of energy in the world, may serve as an example. It has thirteen hundred years' worth of coal, nineteen years' worth of oil, twenty-four years' worth of oil shale (a form of rock containing oil, but not yet widely used as a fuel source), and sixty-three years' worth of natural gas. When these reserves of fossil fuels have been exhausted, no other reserves will remain in this country. Some other form of energy will have to be found if this nation is to continue to operate its machines as it has in the past.

Fortunately, some other possibilities exist. One of them is water, which is used to generate large amounts of the electricity distributed in the United States. Water provides energy as it is drawn downhill by gravity. By storing the natural runoff of mountain streams in reservoirs high above sea level and then releasing it to power plants at lower altitudes, man can use the force of water to turn electric generators. Depending on the height at which the water is first captured, its power can be used and reused several times. Once it reaches sea level, however, its power (actually the force of gravity) is lost, except for the movement of ocean water by the tides, which are caused by the gravitational pull of the moon on the earth. Tidal energy has been suggested as a means of generating electricity, but few successful ways of using it for this purpose have yet been found.

The fissioning of the radioactive elements uranium and plutonium is also being developed as an energy source. Plutonium is an element that does not occur naturally on the earth; it must first be manufactured from uranium in atomic reactors, but the earth has enough uranium for about a thousand years at present rates of use. When the atoms of these two elements are bombarded with neutrons, atomic particles without an electrical charge, the elements are broken apart, or fissioned. Each fissioning atom yields energy. Fission energy can be used to heat water into steam, and the steam can then be used to turn steam turbines. They, in turn, will move generators to produce electricity.

The gasification of coal, a complicated chemical process that converts coal into natural gas, is another, as yet untested, way in which man may gain new supplies of energy. By mixing coal, the most plentiful of the fossil fuels, with certain chemicals under intense heat and pressure, scientists can convert coal into methane gas. The gas can then be burned more efficiently than coal itself. Gasification is still a laboratory process, but it is now being studied as a way to create new energy.

When all of man's fossil fuels have been exhausted, he will have to turn to the sun, his ultimate source of energy. The sun releases energy through the direct radiation that it showers upon the earth's surface each day as heat and light. Such radiation is only a tiny portion of the total daily energy output of the sun, but even this small amount goes unused on the earth's surface, except for that captured by green plants.

If solar radiation could be concentrated through focusing mirrors or photoelectric cells, it, too, could yield useful power for mankind. Until recently scientists have made little effort to develop either of these two methods because of the abundance of fossil fuels, but as they disappear, more and more attention will be directed toward these potential sources of energy.

The sun also makes energy through the thermonuclear process. Deep inside the sun, hydrogen gas, the most abundant element in our star, is subjected to tremendous heat and pressure that fuses hydrogen atoms together to make helium atoms. In the process each combination releases a small amount of energy. Billions upon billions of hydrogen atoms are burned in this way each day, creating the sun's light and heat. As the thermonuclear reactions create heat, it flows to the sun's surface and is freed into space. Man has duplicated this reaction on earth for milliseconds by exploding hydrogen bombs. His hope is that he will be able to create and sustain much longer fusion reactions from which to draw new energy. Yet despite more than twenty years of experimentation, thermonuclear power is still not a reality. The great difficulty in attempting it is the creation of a container capable of holding the reacting hydrogen atoms together. The tremendous heat and pressure make it impossible to use any conventional container. Most experimental containers have been magnetic "bottles," powerful lines of magnetic force shaped to hold the fusion reaction. These deform easily, however, and a successful thermonuclear reactor has yet to be built.

Until man develops new sources of energy, he will face a mounting power crisis, a threefold emergency: the depletion of existing fossil fuel reserves, a constantly mounting demand for energy to power growing numbers of machinery, and an ever more rapidly increasing human population.

The multiplication of man will also have its effect on his other important energy source, food. Man must have food from which to extract the energy he needs for his body. He may be able to survive without fossil fuels, but he cannot hope to live without food, now unevenly distributed across the earth's surface. Some food, notably fish, is gathered wild, but most of man's food supply now comes from domesticated plants and animals. They supply the substances needed to keep the machinery of the body in operation, but they vary in availability from country to country around the world. In technologically developed nations great quantities of food are grown. In other parts of the world hardly enough food is harvested to feed the growing population. Famine has been averted in the underdeveloped countries of the world largely because more fortunate nations have shared their surpluses.

The gap between the amount of food man grows and the amount he needs was first recognized in the eighteenth century by an English economist and clergyman, Thomas Malthus. In his now famous book *An Essay on the Principle of Population,* Malthus pointed out that like other species man increases in number geometrically; that is, at a constantly rising ratio (two, four, eight, sixteen, etc.), while the growing of food can be increased only numerically. If this is true, Malthus said, then mankind will always increase at a rate greater than existing food supplies will increase. Darwin incorporated this portion of Malthus' writings into his own views of the adaptation of species to ecological niches, using it to explain why nature produced more of a species than could possibly survive on the food available.

Since the time of Malthus and Darwin, other scientists have applied the same principle to man. There is, however, an important difference between man's food-gathering ability and that of other species. Man is able to modify the conditions under which food is grown and, by so doing, increase his food production, a skill other forms of life do not have. Other species do store food from season to season—although seldom beyond a year—but they are unable to plant and reap, to breed and slaughter, as man does. It remains an open question as to whether or not man tends to increase his food production whenever he increases his numbers, or whether increases in the amount of food merely encourage the birth of more and more human beings.

Man's population problems stem from other factors as well. His control of disease is one of the most important. To maintain a stable population, any species must have approximately the same number of deaths as births in any given period of time. Discoveries in medicine and science have helped man to live longer, but at the same time the birth rate has gone up. The result is an average increase of births over deaths of about 140,000 human beings a day. This figure, multiplied by the days of the year, brings the average yearly increase in the world's human population to more than fifty million persons.

That alone would be unfortunate, but the problem is

made more serious because the increase is not evenly divided among the nations of the earth. Those countries least able to improve their food production have the largest increases in population. This can only result in both local and worldwide scarcities of man's most vital energy source, food.

The increase in man's population has had two important effects on man. It has increased human pollution of the biosphere and permanently altered the natural landscape. As man multiplies and requires more and more fuel, he also increases the amount of waste he discharges into the air and water. Any energetic reaction produces some pollution, even so simple an act as lighting a match. Multiplied a billionfold, this discharge of wastes into the biosphere threatens to engulf our planet in garbage.

Pollution has always been a part of man's existence, but during his early history, its effect on the earth was minute. Early man's wastes consisted of a few bones, some stone hammers, axes, grinding stones, and charred pieces of wood. Human sewage also was produced, but it was rapidly degraded by the forces of the natural world and recycled back into the earth. Not until men began to gather in cities did garbage and sewage become a peculiarly human problem. Even the ancient cities of the Middle East, the first to be built, contained garbage dumps. By the time of the Roman Empire, sewage had become enough of a problem in large cities to require sewer systems. In the Dark Ages, which followed the collapse of Rome, man's interest in sewage declined, unfortunately for him. The Black Death, an outbreak of bubonic plague carried by the rats that infested garbage in the Middle Ages, was the result. It killed a quarter of the population of Europe.

By the nineteenth century, as industrialization spread through Europe and reached the United States, garbage and sewage became an ever greater problem. As the wastes of industrial civilization spread out over Europe and parts of the United States, streams, lakes, and the land itself became polluted. Sewer systems were built and garbage dumps created away from the cities, but still the torrent of waste products poured out over the land. The Black Country of central England, sooty with coal dust and smoke, became a horrible example of the uncontrolled wasting of the natural landscape.

Reform of the system did not really begin until the twentieth century, when men came to understand that the industrial civilization of the earth was creating wastes more rapidly than they could be recycled back into biologically useful substances. The problem is not only too much waste, but also the forms in which it is dumped into the biosphere. Some, like paper and plastic, cannot be degraded into biological substances without the expenditure of large amounts of energy. Others, like human sewage, must be treated, again with the use of additional energy, before they can be turned into fertilizers and other useful materials. Even as waste and garbage mount, man struggles to find ways to use them successfully.

More subtle and even less well understood is the pollution of the biosphere that heat itself can cause. As man burns more and more fuel for energy, he releases more and more heat into the atmosphere—and sometimes into water. No one yet knows a safe limit to place on such pollution but it is obvious that the air is measurably warmer over cities than it is over rural countryside. Whether heat accumulates in the atmosphere is uncertain. The earth, however, has been both warmer and colder in the past. Some scientists have suggested that large dumping of heat into the atmosphere may eventually cause the same "greenhouse effect" that brought severe changes in the earth's weather in the past. Too much heat may cause an accumulation of carbon dioxide in the atmosphere. This may have the effect of trapping additional heat, which, in turn, might cause the condensation of more water into snow and rain, raising the level of the oceans, melting the polar ice caps, and eroding the continents into the seas.

While heat pollution is an unknown factor, man does know that the widespread and increasing use of the internal-combustion engine in automobiles has dumped hydrocarbons, nitrogen oxides, and other parts of smog into the air in and around cities. Leaded gasolines also place that element in the air, where the rain catches it and carries it to the earth's surface. The damage that is done to humans, plants, and other life by automobile exhaust emissions is as uncertain as how such emissions may eventually be controlled. No suitable substitute for the gasoline-powered internal-combustion engine has yet been developed. The number of automobiles in use in the world continues to grow, and most efforts at solving the problem have concentrated on controlling exhaust gases, rather than controlling the number of engines producing them.

A second major effect of the increase in man's numbers is his alteration of the natural features of the planet. Roadways, cities, canals, dams, power lines, and a host of other man-made structures have gradually encroached on the landscape, changing its appearance, destroying other life forms, and so domesticating the world that man has been forced to set aside certain areas as parks to preserve the natural wilderness from disappearing completely. The effect of such change on man has been both physical and psychological. He has become so separated from nature that he tends to believe he is no longer a part of it.

Man thus seems to be caught in an ascending spiral of circumstances. He continues to grow in number. To feed such numbers, he needs more and more machines. To fuel new machines, he must exhaust his remaining supplies of energy. By using his machines he increases his pollution of the natural earth and his separation from it. The only asset he has that might help him is his brain. Man takes for granted that his ability to think and gather knowledge will be sufficient to get him out of the dilemma he is in, yet he really does not know. His knowledge about himself and his world is a slender thread that ends with the beginning of recorded history. A lapse of two or three generations might so separate him from his past that he could not survive.

Such a gap in human evolution has happened once in man's history. When Rome fell fifteen hundred years ago and with it the knowledge assembled in both Greece and Rome, Europe descended into a dark age from which there seemed no exit. Only because the sum of ancient learning had been written down and preserved in a few libraries was Western man able once again to emerge into the light and hope of the Renaissance.

It is to escape that fate, to prevent the coming of a new reign of darkness, that man must somehow remake himself. If he does not, the descent from his continuing upward journey, begun so laboriously and so long ago in the Ice Ages, may become permanent.

8

Decreasing Numbers

One day in 1943 an American biochemist, Russell E. Marker, walked into a chemical laboratory in Mexico City. In his arms he carried two glass jars wrapped in newspaper, containing four and a half pounds of *progesterone,* a female hormone. However, the progesterone in Dr. Marker's jars had not come from women, but from the roots of a yam, *cabeza de negro,* which grows wild in Mexican jungles. The yam had brought Marker to Mexico from Pennsylvania, where he had been teaching biochemistry. It contained *sapogenins,* substances similar in molecular structure to progesterone. Marker had worked out a process by which he could convert sapogenins to progesterone and other female hormones.

Progesterone, even in those days, was a molecule of interest to biochemists because it could be used to regulate women's menstrual cycles. Although all the chemical steps were not yet understood, biochemists and biomedical researchers knew that some women did not secrete enough progesterone to bring about regular monthly menstrual periods. Regular menstruation is often necessary to aid women who wish to conceive children, and a pill containing progesterone might bring about that regularity.

Some female.hormones had already been isolated by 1943, mostly in Europe and largely from human urine, sows' ovaries, and the adrenal glands of cattle. No one had yet found a way to make large amounts of synthetic progesterone, however, and the material in Marker's two jars represented a major part of the refined hormone then existing in the world. Using a makeshift laboratory, he had managed to work out a series of complicated steps by which the sapogenins in yam roots could be converted into progesterone.

The company to which Marker took his two jars that day was run by two naturalized Mexican citizens of European extraction, Emeric Somlo and Federico Lehmann. After listening to Marker and examining the material in his jars, they agreed to set up a new firm, Syntex, S.A., to manufacture more progesterone. A year and a half later Marker, after a dispute with his partners, quit, taking with him the record of how he had managed to synthesize progesterone. To continue his work, Somlo and Lehmann hired George Rosenkranz, a Hungarian chemist then living in Cuba. Within a few years Rosenkranz was able to synthesize more progesterone from yam roots, although his method was different from that used by Marker. He also was able to synthesize the male hormone *testosterone*, and several other steroids.

A few years later, in 1949, Rosenkranz was joined by a brilliant young American chemist, Carl Djerassi. Together the two produced two more synthetic estrogens, *estrone* and *estradiol*. At first the substances were used only to regulate menstrual cycles in women, but because of this, they helped add to the knowledge scientists were gathering about ovulation, which is the production of a fertile *ovum*, or egg cell.

Menstruation begins in puberty. It is the result of a complicated series of biochemical reactions ending when the ovaries release egg cells into the Fallopian tubes, where they may be fertilized by sperm ejaculated by males as a part of semen during sexual intercourse. The release of eggs in the female begins when the hypothalamus in the brain signals the nearby pituitary gland to secrete a protein hormone called *follicle-stimulating hormone* (FSH). After its release from the pituitary, FSH travels through the bloodstream to the ovaries. There it stimulates the growth of a *follicle*, a small, capsulelike bit of tissue, which emerges on the surface of the ovary and in which the female egg is formed.

At the same time, the pituitary also secretes another hormone called *luteinizing hormone* (LH). This substance, also traveling through the bloodstream, causes the follicle to begin making estrogen. The estrogen, in turn, acts on the lining of the uterus, or womb—where any embryo will develop from a fertilized egg cell—preparing it for that possibility. A few days later, after the follicle has been fully developed, estrogen, also traveling through the blood, reaches the pituitary and apparently orders it to step up its production of LH. The new supply of LH then travels back to the follicle and causes it to break open, releasing the egg cell it contains for passage into the Fallopian tube. LH also converts the now ruptured follicle into a gland, the *corpus luteum*, which begins to secrete progesterone. Progesterone stimulates further growth of the lining of the uterus, but at the same time, it begins to build up in the body and eventually stops the production of LH—just how is not known. If enough progesterone accumulates in the body, as it does when pregnancy happens, then *all* secretion of FSH and LH is stopped until birth is over.

This last fact was of great interest to biochemical

research workers, for it meant that if they could stimulate the body to produce sufficiently high levels of progesterone and estrogen, or if they could supply it with enough of these two hormones, they might be able to prevent the ovaries from making any follicles or egg cells at all. (This is what happens in pregnancy when their production stops.)

With this goal in mind, Djerassi, Rosenkranz, and a number of scientists in other countries began looking for a way to make synthetic hormones that would have the same effect as naturally secreted progesterone when taken by mouth. All during the 1950's they worked on the problem, and finally they succeeded in creating two similar substances, *northindrone* and *norethyndreal.* They also made a third substance, *mestranol,* a synthetic biochemical similar to estradiol. When the two compounds were combined, they became the first successful oral contraceptive.

Interest in the development of an oral contraceptive had increased after World War II because of awakening recognition of the world's growing population problem. Even then it was clear that human beings were multiplying faster than ever before in history. The reason for this rapid rise in population was then, as now, not completely understood, but it seemed certain that some cheap, effective method of birth control was needed if the brakes were to be applied to the worldwide race between new mouths and available food.

Both artificial and "natural" contraception had been used before World War II. Indeed artificial contraception is a very ancient practice. In ancient times—and even today in some primitive societies—many substances have been used after sexual intercourse in an attempt to prevent the fertilization of egg cells by sperm. These were to prevent conception in the female, and they ranged from foam from a camel's mouth to seaweed.

The only successful male contraceptive device was developed a few hundred years ago in England when the intestines of sheep were cleaned, dried, and fashioned into *condoms*. Fitted over an erect penis, sheep condoms prevented semen ejaculated during sexual intercourse from reaching female egg cells. Condoms of sheep intestine were far too expensive for the average male, however, and it was not until the invention of vulcanized rubber by Charles Goodyear in the nineteenth century that mass-produced rubber condoms were possible. Today more than 700 million of them are sold in the United States each year.

Males, even in ancient times, also practiced withdrawal, the removal of the penis from the vagina before ejaculation, as a means of contraception. The condom, however, remains the only successful artificial method of contraception for males.

The invention of vulcanized rubber also led to the development of the *diaphragm*, a thin sheet of rubber or, now, plastic fitted over a round ring, made either of metal or rubber. The diaphragm is inserted in the vagina and fitted tightly over the mouth of the uterus to prevent the union of sperm and egg cells.

A third and recent female contraceptive device is the *intrauterine device*, or IUD, a thin curled spiral of plastic, sometimes called the *Lippes loop*, because it was perfected by Dr. Jack Lippes, an American physician. The device is inserted in the uterus, often for long periods of time. Why it prevents pregnancy is not known, but it apparently makes it impossible for fertilized eggs to implant themselves in the uterus. Instead, they are carried away and leave the body during menstruation. In the United States the IUD must be inserted by a physician to avoid the danger of uterine infection.

A variety of foams, jellies, tablets, and other chemicals also have been developed as contraceptive devices. Usually they work by destroying the sperm or making it nonviable after it has entered the vagina. All are inconvenient to use because they must be applied immediately before sexual intercourse.

In addition to these methods of contraception, two operations also permanently prevent pregnancy from happening: *vasectomy*, the tying off of the *vas deferens*, the tubes which in males lead from the testicles, where sperm cells are formed, to the penis; and *sterilization*, the tying off of the Fallopian tubes, to keep the egg cells from entering the uterus and to prevent the passage of sperm cells into the Fallopian tubes. If conception has occurred, there is *abortion*, the removal of an embryo or fetus from the uterus, either by scraping or sucking it away from the uterine wall.

Of the three operations, abortion has caused the most controversy. Long illegal in the United States, except under unusual circumstances where birth might endanger the mother or the unborn child, it has recently gained growing acceptance. Beginning in the 1960's many states passed laws relaxing their rules against abortion, and in 1973 the United States Supreme Court held that abortion is a woman's right, if she wishes it. The ruling, however, includes a time schedule under which abortion can be legally performed. The schedule seems to mean that all abortions are legally possible with a woman's consent during the first three months of pregnancy, permissible under certain circumstances during the second three months of pregnancy, and illegal, except under unusual circumstances, during the last three months of pregnancy. The practical effect of the ruling, however, is to permit abortion if it is requested by a woman.

Abortion also remains illegal in many countries where the Catholic religion is practiced by the majority of the population, because the Catholic Church is opposed to both abortion and artificial contraception. Catholic belief holds that life begins at the moment of conception, rather than at the moment of birth. Catholics thus view both artificial contraception and abortion as the denial of life to a soul and, in effect, murder. The Church, however, does permit contraception through abstention from sexual relations during the time of the menstrual cycle when a women's egg cell is most likely to be fertilized. This system, often called the *rhythm method*, is supposed to be based on the natural rhythms of life.

Although no method of contraception, except sterilization, absolutely guarantees the prevention of pregnancy and birth, the oral contraceptive remains the safest, easiest, and most successful. The success of oral contraceptives depends on their being taken once every day for twenty or twenty-one days beginning with the fifth day after the onset of menstruation. Oral contraceptives are available in two forms. The first and oldest is a pill containing both progesterone and estradiol or mestranol. The second, a sequential oral contraceptive, consists of fifteen pills of estrogen only, followed by a series of pills containing both estrogen and a progesterone. Sequential pills are thought by some doctors to mimic the natural secretion of female hormones more successfully. Both kinds of pills raise the level of hormones in a woman's body until it is high enough to prevent the formation of follicles and egg cells.

Despite the success with which present oral contraceptives work, they do have some disadvantages. A few women may develop side effects, sometimes serious ones, from their use, although whether the pill is to blame is still a matter of medical dispute. Even though pills cost only a few pennies a day, they are still too expensive to be of much use in many of the poorer nations of the world. Moreover, if they are to be used successfully, they should be accompanied by instruction and education. In nations where few can read or write, this is difficult. Finally, like all contraceptive devices, their success depends on acceptance by their users. Acceptance often is difficult or impossible where a man's virility, wealth, social status, or success is measured by the number of children he can father. The opposition to their use, or the use of any contraceptive, in Catholic countries, especially South America, is also a major barrier.

In countries where oral contraceptives are too expensive, the IUD sometimes is used as a substitute. It is cheaper over a long period of time. Like the oral contraceptive, however, it has certain disadvantages in mass use. A minority of women either cannot wear the IUD or are so irritated by it that it must be removed. Also, IUD's should be installed under as sterile conditions as possible by trained health workers. Many countries have too few physicians and health workers as it is. Training new teams in the proper insertion of the IUD could be as difficult as attempting to educate women in the use of oral contraceptives.

The lack of trained physicians poses the same problem with abortions. They should be performed by doctors or carefully trained medical workers, but few countries with large populations have medical or nursing schools where such training can take place. Again, until or unless the Catholic Church withdraws its opposition to this method of population control, abortion seems unlikely to be adopted widely.

Yet population control of some kind seems essential for the world, if it is to avoid "natural methods" of limiting increases in human numbers—that is, disease, social disorder, war, and political upheaval. Within the next twenty-five years the population of a majority of the nations in Asia, Africa, and South America will double, if the present rate of increase is maintained. In only a few countries—Austria and Ireland, for example—is population at a stable level. In these "zero population" nations, growth is controlled by special factors: emigration to other countries, the lack of economic opportunity, marriage at a late age, and other economic and social controls on family size.

It is, of course, man's decision as to whether he will limit his numbers or allow them to be limited by natural forces. If he decides to attempt the job himself, he must decide soon on the methods he is going to use. Much present discussion of population control is based on the assumption that wanting to control the population will be enough and that voluntary controls will work. Some population experts, however, believe voluntary controls alone will not do the job. They say eventually compulsory national or international regulation of population will be necessary to avoid natural disaster.

Nevertheless, involuntary control of population may be even more difficult than the voluntary use of artificial contraceptive devices. Compulsory control of population

invades one of man's most basic privacies, sexual intercourse, and challenges one of his most treasured freedoms,
the freedom to reproduce himself. Compulsory population
control will have to contend not only with social and
religious forces, but also with one of man's greatest
dreams, his desire for immortality through his children
and his family. Perhaps because of all these things, no
nation on earth has yet attempted involuntary population
control, and no one really knows if it can successfully be
carried out.

Clearly, however, if voluntary control does not work,
compulsory control of some kind will be forced on the
world, either by man or by nature. Human control of the
population may include all the present methods of artificial contraception, including abortion, but it may also
require drugs and devices not yet invented. In addition
it may require political control through the passage of
special laws governing the size of families.

One such suggested measure would limit all newly
married couples to only two children. The law might
require each couple who is marrying to obtain not only
a marriage license, but also a license to have children.
Most estimates give an average of two children per each
married couple as the number necessary to balance births
and deaths and achieve zero population growth. Under
such a law, couples could have their two children, or they
could sell their license to another couple who wished to
have more than two. Couples with two children might
be allowed to adopt unwanted children too. A couple that
conceived a child beyond the legal limit might be subject
to a heavy fine, one that would grow progressively larger
with each new child added to the family beyond the legal
two. In effect, the law would substitute an artificial

financial barrier for "natural" economic conditions, which tend to limit births.

The nation's birthrate parallels the rise and fall of its economic health. For instance, fewer children are born when times are hard, as during the Depression of the 1930's. An exception to this rule was 1972, when the birthrate in the United States dropped to its lowest level since the 1930's, in spite of a healthy economy.

Could a law limiting family size be passed in a democratically ruled nation? And would it really be effective in limiting population? No one believes it will be easy. Perhaps it would be less difficult in nations without elected governments such as Russia, where abortions were encouraged at will after the Russian Revolution in the 1920's and then discouraged after World War II, when the population dropped sharply.

Beyond political controls lie new and as yet untried biological methods of preventing conception. Sometimes called second-generation contraceptives, most of them are modifications of present oral contraceptives, IUD's, or drugs. A second-generation oral contraceptive already on the market is the "mini-pill," a drug without synthetic estrogen, made only of a progestogen. The progestogen apparently prevents sperm from reaching egg cells by aiding mucus formation at the mouth of the uterus. This keeps sperm from moving up the oviducts to egg cells released by the ovaries. While the mini-pill has fewer side effects than first-generation pills, it also has a higher "failure rate"; that is, it is less likely to prevent pregnancy.

Modification of the IUD includes changing its shape to make it easier for women to wear and the addition of small amounts of chemicals, usually progesterone, to the materials of which the IUD is made. These chemicals are slowly released into the uterus to affect its lining, but they do not migrate to other parts of the body, where they might cause undesirable side effects. Although the device is still being tested, it may offer contraception for up to one year.

Other long-term contraceptive devices being tested are an implantable capsule, which could be inserted under the skin, and a ring inserted in the vagina. In either place, the device could release hormones slowly to prevent the fertilization of egg cells. The vaginal ring would have to be removed every month to allow menstruation to take place, but the implantable capsule might last as long as a year. An injectable contraceptive capable of preventing pregnancy for as long as three months is being tested in Europe.

In the United States the Food and Drug Administration in 1973 licensed a "morning after" pill, a substance to prevent pregnancy after, rather than before, sexual intercourse. The pill, made of diethylstilbestrol (DES), is too dangerous to use regularly as a contraceptive and is to be given only when rape or incest might cause pregnancy.

Physicians are also experimenting with two new versions of vasectomy and sterilization. Both operations, as now performed, permanently close the openings through which sperm and egg cells are normally released. Surgeons are now testing plastic valves, which could be inserted in the *vas deferens* in men, and plastic plugs, which might temporarily close the Fallopian tubes. The valves and plugs could be removed at a later time when pregnancy was desired.

Two researchers are also exploring a way of making the rhythm method more precise. Contraception by this method depends on sexual intercourse occurring only when ovulation is not taking place. However, women often have difficulty in telling exactly when or when not to engage in sexual relations. Roger Guillemin of the Salk Institute in San Diego and Andrew Schally of the New Orleans Veterans Administration Hospital are studying the *luteinizing hormone releasing hormone* (LH-RH), the hormone secreted by the hypothalamus which orders, in turn, the secretion of LH by the pituitary gland. LH-RH already has been made synthetically in the laboratory, and the two research workers are now seeking a way to block its action synthetically. If they could, they might be able to start and stop ovulation with great precision, making certain the days when a woman is ovulating and producing eggs cells capable of being fertilized by sperm.

Erwin Goldberg of Northwestern University is studying ways to stimulate antibodies that might suppress the action of either sperm or egg cells, thus offering the hope that a male oral contraceptive may someday be discovered. Although several different kinds of female contraceptive pills have been discovered, male contraception by chemical means is still not possible.

No matter how many drugs are developed for contraception, any program of population control, whether voluntary or involuntary, must, in the end, depend on education and improvement in mass communication. It must also be preceded by an understanding among nations and peoples that a world with too many people in it is an impossible world in which to live. To the poor, the uneducated, and the illiterate this goal—a world with fewer rather than more persons in it—seems of little importance. Those who most need to limit their families' size in Asia, Africa, and South America have other needs that seem far more important to them in the daily struggle to find enough to eat, a place to live, and the ability to think beyond survival.

Where population control has been attempted—in India, for example, where the population increases by a million persons a month—those who accept birth-control devices, sterilization, and other kinds of contraception are usually people who already have as many children as they want. Therefore, their agreement to contraception comes too late and has little real effect on the total increase in human numbers. To such families and nations an appeal for understanding of the problem must be made in ways not being used today.

At the same time, the wealthy nations of the world, even though they may voluntarily limit their population, cannot expect poorer nations to follow their example until the underdeveloped areas of the world have enough to eat. Ironically, a limit to the population makes little sense to those who already are limited by a lack of food, clothing, shelter, and the other necessities of life.

Despite these problems, there is some reason for hope. India has adopted a national program of population control. China, after finding it had a hundred million more citizens than it thought, has begun birth-control efforts. Scattered attacks on the problem are also being made in South America and Africa.

Japan is the nation with the most experience in national efforts at population control. The Japanese began a national drive to control population growth after the end of World War II, when they realized they could no longer depend on overseas emigration to ease population pressures in their home islands. Oral contraceptives were not yet available, but abortion, to which there were no

religious barriers, was. The Japanese government encouraged abortion. Then as oral contraceptives were
perfected, the use of abortion as a means of preventing
birth declined.

By such efforts, the Japanese were able to cut the rate
of their population increase in half in the 1950's and early
1960's. However, the Japanese, like the Russians, discovered that a sudden reduction in births brings with it
new problems. As births declined, so did the number of
young people entering the labor market. Japan, a highly
developed nation technologically, was faced with severe
labor shortages as older workers retired or died and could
not be replaced by younger people. After that the Japanese relaxed their efforts at population control, and today
their rate of population increase is again on the rise.

Few countries in Asia, Africa, or South America have
too few workers. Instead, their problem is to achieve rapid
technological development, to train new workers in skills
they have never before possessed, to build new machines
and factories, to find the energy and raw materials with
which to manufacture goods and, in general, to catch up
with Europe and North America. Their problem in population control is one of planning.

In the end, population control for all nations means
population planning. Limiting population, even *attempting* to limit population, is more than simply wanting to
do so. It also means understanding the reasons for population increase and the ways in which controls can be fitted
to different ways of life.

The most crucial of man's decisions today concerns the
control of human life—and death. Much has already
been done to delay death. Indeed, man's success in
reducing the world's death rate in all countries is the chief

reason for the present crisis in numbers. Man now needs to apply the lessons he has learned in limiting death to the limiting of life—before death itself does so.

Man's failure to control his numbers will lead only to their control by means beyond man's powers: epidemics of disease, new national and international wars, and social disorder and chaos, which will either cripple or end man's rule as the dominant species of the earth.

9

Dwellers Among the Tombs

"I think, therefore I am," Descartes said, meaning that man is an organism with a brain, but that he is also a being equipped with something more, a mind and a *self*, a being similar to all his species, yet somehow uniquely and endlessly different. Throughout his existence, man has struggled with this paradox. Each of us thinks of himself as an individual, yet we know too that we look, act, talk, and are like other men. In the end each of us is forced to conclude that the difference between himself and all others is his own deep, interior collection of knowledge and feelings which he alone completely knows. This inner reservoir remains mankind's least understood, least charted frontier. It may also be our most important asset in survival. It governs not only how we feel about ourselves, but also how we deal with the world outside our body. Man's life is a constant effort to balance these two worlds—one within, the other without.

The way man compromises with the contending forces of self and the world is measured by behavior. Behavior is the reaction between the self and the information it receives from the senses. We are angry, sad, happy, or apathetic not only because of the things that happen around us, but also because of the effect they have on the collection of experiences that makes up our own par-

ticular, unique self. Man's ability to behave collectively
—that is, with other men—is his greatest advantage over
other forms of life. It is also his greatest burden, because
although it permits his cooperation with his fellows, it
makes him aggressive as well.

Yet although we understand this much about the mind
and the self, much more remains uncertain. Where, for
example, are the "mind" and the "self" located? Are they
in some physical place in the brain? If so, can we trace
their patterns? And, if we can, can we thus control the
individual?

Almost a hundred years ago a Viennese physician,
Sigmund Freud, pondered these questions. Freud's interest in the self arose from his concern for those who were
sick of mind and exhibited abnormal behavior. Freud was
concerned with the reasons for such behavior. He knew
it is difficult to measure behavior. It cannot be done by
looking at the brain, but rather in noticing how the brain
causes the body to act. Freud believed abnormal behavior might indicate that the mind was sick. Often those
whose behavior is abnormal are called crazy or insane,
but Freud realized that abnormal behavior could also take
less drastic forms. He contended that mental illness could
be cured, not by physical medicine, but by exploring the
reasons for the unusual behavior.

Freud was not the first to consider the mind or brain
as an organ capable of treatment. Centuries before, the
writers of the Gospels in the New Testament had recorded
an instance of mental illness and its cure (Luke 8:26–33).

So they landed in the country of the Gergesenes, which
is opposite Galilee. As he stepped ashore, he was met by a
man from the town who was possessed of the devils. For

a long time he had neither worn clothes nor lived in a house, but stayed among the tombs. When he saw Jesus, he cried out and fell at his feet shouting, "What do you want with me, Jesus, son of the Most High God? I implore you, do not torment me."

For Jesus was already ordering the unclean spirit to come out of the man. Many a time it had seized him, and then, for safety's sake, they would secure him with chains and fetters; but each time he broke loose and with the devil in charge made off to the solitary places.

Jesus asked him, "What is your name?" "Legion," he replied. This was because so many devils had taken possession of him. And they begged him not to banish them to the Abyss.

There happened to be a large herd of pigs nearby, feeding on the hill; and the spirits begged him to let them go into these pigs. He gave them leave; the devils came out of the man and went into the pigs, and the herd rushed over the edge into the lake and were drowned.

In the centuries since Christ's time those who behaved abnormally were seldom treated as was the man whose name was Legion. Instead, the mentally ill were made social outcasts, ignored as hopeless fools, or imprisoned in asylums, places often equal to, or worse than, jails.

Freud believed this need not be so. He attempted to gather information from the minds of the mentally ill through a system he called *psychoanalysis*. Freud suggested that the mind could be divided into three areas: the *id*, a vast collection of experience, different for each individual, which was always held below the level of conscious thought; the *ego*, that part of the mind which expressed itself in conscious behavior; and the *superego*, a control that separated the conscious from the subconscious, permitting only certain thoughts to appear in the conscious mind.

Freud contended that the mind, if properly instructed, could be controlled, ending mental illness. He believed such a cure was possible by carefully examining the contents of the id. If, he said, a trained *therapist*, a person able to treat the mind, could bring a mentally ill person to the point where he could recall his past at random, this free association of memories could explain, first to the therapist, and then to the patient, why he was acting as he was. With the aid of this insight into the patient's troubles, controls could be fashioned that would prevent him from behaving abnormally in the future.

This, of course, is a greatly simplified explanation of psychoanalysis. Freudian psychology is much more complicated, and it would be difficult to explain it in detail in this book. Freud believed, for example, that human behavior is the result of sexual drive, for the most part, and that much of one's personality or self is bound up in one's childhood relations with one's mother and father. Freud also was interested in dreams and hypnosis. He thought dreams were symbols for the contents of the subconscious and that hypnosis was another way of reaching the self.

Many variations of Freud's methods followed his discovery of psychoanalysis. Present-day investigators of the mind have modified or discarded many of his ideas, yet all retain the belief that there is a human mind, that it can become sick, and that it can be controlled. The belief that the mind can be controlled is perhaps Freud's most lasting contribution to mankind. Before his time men often had been physically forced to accept ideas, but the control of the individual mind itself was considered impossible. By suggesting that the mind could be sick and might be made well again, Freud also brought up the possibility that the mind could be altered and controlled by others.

Freud's writings led others to accept the idea that behavior is the way in which the self expresses both conscious and subconscious thought to the world. The study of behavior became an accepted way to control the individual self. Behaviorists, however, came to differ widely on how control is to be carried out. In general, their theories fall into two large groups. The first revolves around the gathering of information from the mind and the use of this information to change behavior. This approach requires the cooperation of the individual being treated and is called *voluntary* behavioral control. The second large group of behavioral theories is based on the assumption that the mind is the sum of the information stored within the brain; that is, it is a physical collection of charged nerve cells. Because it is a physical entity, it can be controlled, so this group of behaviorists says, by physical means—drugs, electrical stimulation, and surgery. This approach implies that the mind can be controlled by *involuntary* means.

Freud probably would have included himself in the first group of behaviorists. He believed the mind and self are a collection of experiences covering most of a person's lifetime, but he thought and wrote before many of the physical means of altering the mind known today were available. He also began his work before the discovery of conditioning.

Conditioning as a means of changing behavior was discovered by two physiologists, one American, the other Russian, while they were studying and working with experimental animals. The most famous of the two experimenters was Ivan P. Pavlov, who is best remembered for his work with dogs. Pavlov's most famous experiment involved placing food before a dog and, at the same time, ringing a bell. The dog salivated when he saw the food. In time he was conditioned to salivate when the bell was rung even though no food was given him. His brain had become conditioned to associating food and the bell. The American psychologist E. L Thorndike performed similar experiments with cats.

Since Pavlov's experiments, an immense amount of conditioning has been done. Rats have been taught to run mazes and pigeons to peck at levers. Conditioning has been developed to modify the behavior of human beings too. Usually, conditioning is useful only for the modification of a single behavior trait. For example, an alcoholic who constantly craves a drink may be cured of his desire to have one if he agrees to experience a weak electric shock each time he reaches for a glass of whiskey. In time he may become so conditioned to the unpleasant sensation of the electric shock that when he sees a drink he will refuse it.

This is called *negative conditioning*, for its success depends on punishment or pain. Conditioning, however, need not be negative. B. F. Skinner, an American behaviorist and author of *Walden Two*, a novel that outlines a Utopian community based on his theories, is a leading advocate of *positive conditioning*. Instead of punishment or pain, the success of positive conditioning depends on reward and the reinforcing of "good" behavior. Skinner contends that children should not be negatively conditioned by being punished for incorrect or unacceptable behavior, but should be rewarded for good behavior instead. Just as a rat can be conditioned to push a lever for a pellet of food, Skinner says, so can a child learn correct behavior through rewards.

Conditioning may be a mixture of positive and negative approaches. Most American children are raised by such a combination of methods. Many behaviorists, however, doubt that conditioning alone either explains or controls all behavior. Apes for example, have been able to stack one box on top of another to reach a banana with no previous conditioning to show them this task, and much human learning and behavior seem to result from whole patterns of experience that suddenly appear in the brain. This view of behavior is called *Gestalt* theory, from the German word *Gestalt*, meaning a configurational whole, or form. Behaviorists do not agree as to whether *Gestalten* themselves can be conditioned in an individual. Most accept the idea that it is sometimes possible to change a single, easily identifiable behavior characteristic through conditioning, but many think a more general control of the self depends on conditioning techniques man does not yet know.

One of the most famous examples of apparent generalized conditioning was that administered to American prisoners during the Korean War. By offering a combination of rewards and punishments to prisoners, their Chinese and North Korean captors apparently were able to "brainwash" them so thoroughly that they approved of enemy, rather than friendly, political beliefs, even after they were released to go home.

The technique was so apparently successful that it became the subject of a novel by Richard Condon, *The Manchurian Candidate*, in which an American prisoner of war is conditioned in captivity to attempt the assassination of the President of the United States when he returns home. Behaviorists doubt that any such behavior modification is possible with present-day conditioning techniques. They also point out that most former prisoners of war rapidly dropped their new political allegiance once they were back in the United States, indicating that conditioning must be constantly reinforced or repeated to create any permanent change in behavior.

Conditioning is important, however, in behavior control, and it has led to new approaches to curing mental illness. One of the newest of these is *action therapy*. In contrast to psychoanalysis, which seeks to give an individual insight into the reasons for his abnormal behavior, action therapy is directed only at the symptoms of abnormality. Action therapists begin with the idea that insight is really not necessary to modify behavior. Instead, they direct some form of action at the symptom. If a child is neither sick nor in pain, there is no reason why he should cry every night when he is put to bed. Yet children often do cry when left by their parents to go to sleep. Repeated visits to their bedsides do nothing to stop their cries. The action therapist's way of controlling this kind of behavior is simply to reassure the child and then leave him alone for the rest of the night. The first night this is attempted, the child may cry for a long time before going to sleep, but the second night the crying usually is much shorter. After several nights, the child goes to sleep without crying at all.

Action therapy also has been used to treat phobias, which are unnatural fears over heights, closed spaces, open spaces, or other normal conditions or situations. Claustrophobia, the fear of closed rooms or spaces, has been treated by placing a sufferer in a tightly fitting sleeping bag in a small, closed area to prove to him that his fears are groundless.

The action therapist may also treat phobias by preparing a list of words (with the help of his patient) that describe, in graded order, the things of which he is afraid. The therapist then flashes pictures of the feared objects or situations on a screen, in the order of the fear they arouse in the patient. Gradually, the patient learns to work his way to the most feared of the objects, ideas, or situations, until he has conquered his phobia. This is called *desensitization* because it gradually makes the patient less and less sensitive to the cause of his problem.

Action therapy may also involve the use of encounter groups, the bringing together of persons unfamiliar with one another to discuss themselves and their problems, usually under the guidance of a trained group leader. By talking over one's troubles with such a group, it is often possible, with the group's help, to reach rapidly into the subconscious, reveal problems, and work out solutions.

Encounter therapy groups vary widely. Some may be marathons, running for three or four days without stopping. Some may involve only couples. Often the members of encounter groups will be brutally frank with one another, while others will attempt only surface discussions of personal behavior. All are voluntary methods of controlling the expression of the self.

Involuntary behavior control involves a much different approach. The involuntary control of behavior has been practiced, in one form or another, for centuries. In ancient times, torture or the threat of torture often forced involuntary changes in behavior, as did death threats or the execution of the individual whose behavior was being modified. The threat of death obviously is the most extreme of controls, and many Americans believe that the threat of execution can successfully modify the behavior of potential murderers and the perpetrators of other violent crimes. Statistics seem to indicate otherwise, however, and capital punishment gradually has declined as a means of attempting to enforce nonviolent behavior in many countries, including the United States.

There are other involuntary methods of behavior control that pose more serious threats to individual freedom. Most of them center around the use of surgery or drugs to control the way people act. This form of involuntary behavior control began in the early years of the twentieth century, when physicians accidentally discovered that large injections of insulin would produce insulin shock in mental patients, sometimes with apparent beneficial results after the patient recovered consciousness. At about the same time, other psychiatrists began using electro-convulsive shock therapy. Electrodes were attached to either side of a patient's skull, and an electric current strong enough to cause muscle contractions and convulsions was then passed through his body. After a series of such treatments, some patients seemed to improve. Psychiatrists were unsure—and remain uncertain—as to why the treatments with either insulin or electricity worked, but many such treatments were given.

At the same time, surgery was used on some patients. To calm disturbed patients, surgeons operated on the brain, cutting down between the front and rear lobes. This operation, called a *prefrontal lobotomy*, was performed on thousands of patients. Although the reason for its apparent modification of the patient's behavior was not clear either, doctors believed that separation of the frontal brain lobes from the hypothalamus may have helped to calm the patients.

Insulin shock, electroconvulsive shock, and prefrontal lobotomies were all abandoned after 1952, when tranquilizing drugs were first introduced in the United States. Chlorpromazine was the first of the strong tranquilizing drugs. Chlorpromazine and a series of derivatives developed since its introduction will reduce violent behavior in mental patients, if the drug is taken regularly. These drugs do nothing organically to change the brain, but they often make it possible for psychiatrists to begin other treatment. Some form of chlorpromazine remains the most widely used method of involuntary behavior control in the treatment of the mentally ill today. Milder drugs also have been developed for less seriously disturbed patients. Some are mild tranquilizers. Others are "energizers," such as methamphetamine, which pep up, rather than tranquilize, an individual.

None of these drugs should be confused with those commonly abused today: marijuana, LSD-25, heroin, cocaine, or similar substances. None of these have any proven medical purpose, and most are either hallucinogens, drugs that separate the individual from reality, or sedatives, which can kill pain at the expense of addiction. There is little understanding of how tranquilizing drugs such as chlorpromazine affect the brain. Even less is understood about hallucinogens such as LSD or marijuana. Many depend for their action on the strength of the dose, the state of mind, and physical condition of the individual taking them, the place and time where they are taken, and other highly variable factors. Much has been written about the use of such substances in the involuntary mass control of behavior, but because so little is known about how they should be given or taken, it is doubtful that they will offer any long-lasting mass control of behavior for years to come. At best, their dangerous side effects and their abuse by inappropriate dose make them a dangerous tool for control of the mind.

A more likely and more frightening prospect for involuntary control of the mind is the use of electrical stimulation. The brain operates because of its minute charges or discharges of electricity, and it clearly can be altered by careful stimulation of the proper neurons with electrical charges. The first electrical stimulation research with the brain began in Germany in 1898, when J. R. Ewald, a professor of physiology, connected an electrical wire to the brain of a dog, sent a current through it, and was able to make the dog perform certain involuntary movements. In 1928 Swiss Nobel Prize winner W. R. Hess used a similar system to make a cat believe it was being attacked. By implanting a wire in the proper place in the cat's brain, Hess could make its hair bristle, its ears flatten, and its eyes dilate, even though no dog was in the room. The cat could also be induced to believe it was hungry, even though it had just been fed.

Since then many experimenters have implanted wires in the brains of laboratory animals. One of the most famous has been Dr. Jose Delgado of Yale University Medical School. Dr. Delgado has been able to plant electrodes in the brain of a bull, force it to charge, and then halt the charge simply by pressing a switch on a radio transmitter, which sends a signal that discharges a small electric current into the bull's thalamus. Dr.

Delgado is working on another system in which a small injector, triggered by radio signals, releases minute amounts of chemicals. They, too, can affect the behavior of an animal. The chemical system, so Dr. Delgado says, is capable of stimulation with much less variation than the electric current.

Other scientists, working with monkeys, have been able to make them perform a whole series of involuntary actions simply by finding the proper places on the surface of the brain for stimulation. Microelectrodes, so small they can be inserted into a single neuron, now make it possible to switch off and on one brain cell at a time.

It is, of course, easier to install an electrical modification in the brain of an experimental animal than it is to do the same thing in a human being. The person's cooperation is required—at least under present laws. Yet surgeons and psychiatrists have electrically stimulated human brains experimentally, inducing both aggressive and non-aggressive behavior. The logical extension of such research is to build a microcomputer (easily possible with the present state of computer technology), surgically install it in the brain, and control it with a radio transmitter at some remote location. Such a system is the theme of Michael Crichton's novel *The Terminal Man*. In the book a psychomotor epileptic, who suffers from involuntary violent behavior, has a small computer installed in his brain that is supposed to modify his aggressive attacks. Unfortunately, the patient overrides the computer and finally has to be killed to keep him from harming others. The prediction of the book, however, remains. Electrical stimulation of the brain, resulting in involuntary behavior changes, could easily become a reality soon.

Some scientists also contend it may be possible to improve the brain, either voluntarily or involuntarily, by the expansion of memory and by the transfer of knowledge from one brain to another, a kind of mental transplant. Such a belief is based, in part, on the experiments of such scientists as Dr. James V. McConnell of the University of Michigan. Dr. McConnell first conditioned *planarians*, a kind of flatworm, by making them crawl a fixed pattern in a maze with the use of strong electric lights and small electric shocks. He then cut up the trained worms and fed them to untrained planarians. The cannibal planarians apparently learned to crawl the maze more rapidly than had the worms they had eaten. They had acquired the memory of the first set of worms.

A similar experiment was performed by Dr. Allan L. Jacobson, a former associate of Dr. McConnell, while at the University of California at Los Angeles. Dr. Jacobson trained rats and hamsters in simple tasks and then extracted brain material from them and injected it into the brains of untrained animals. The injected rats and hamsters seemed to learn the same tasks more rapidly than had the first group of animals. The difference in learning time seemed to be greater even when rat brain material was injected into hamsters and vice versa.

These experiments seem to indicate that memory is, in some way, a function of the RNA in neurons—but just how remains unclear. When, however, older persons with faulty memories receive injections of RNA material extracted from young people, their memory seems to improve. It is uncertain whether memory is transcribed in some way in RNA or whether additional RNA simply makes it easier for neurons to retain information.

Computers also offer a way to improve brain function

and to expand the use of the mind. They may also assist man in behavior control. Computers have been called thinking machines, but when they do calculations they are really only using systems prepared for them by thinking men. Computers can often do such calculations much more rapidly than men, however, and it has been suggested that they may eventually be programmed to reproduce themselves by assembling components into systems. Since their invention, computers have been built with greater and greater capacity to store information. Although no present-day computer can yet approach the memory capacity of a human brain, nor its compact size, their ability to simulate human thinking grows increasingly refined with time.

The great difficulty with computers is finding ways in which to enter and extract information. The human brain receives many more "inputs" and returns many more bits of information each minute than is possible even with the newest and best computers. Most present-day computers must be fed information in a *linear* fashion—that is, much as one views a motion picture, a frame at a time. The human brain, however, seems able to act on several different levels at the same time, and its information is "read out" at once in a series of different complex expressions that we call behavior. Computers seem incapable of this variability of expression.

This does not mean man may not someday be able to communicate with a computer almost as directly as he does with the memory banks of his own brain, directly and on several different levels at once. When that is possible, man may be able to create a kind of extension of himself, a kind of auxiliary brain that will greatly expand his individual thinking capacity. This new warehouse of information will remain outside his body, open to examination, change, and repair in a way the brain is not. Unfortunately, it will also be much more open to manipulation by others or by other computers, a prospect that is at once exciting and frightening. Such a situation is an important sequence in the film *Space Odyssey 2001*. In it, Hal, the computer that operates a spaceship traveling to Jupiter, almost manages to take over control of the humans on the ship, too, and finally has to be dismantled by the craft's only survivor.

Thus the promise and threat of computer auxiliaries to the brain raises the question central to all human behavior control, whether voluntary or involuntary: Who is to be in charge? Who is to be the master controller? Until now, behavior controls have been prepared, often in a haphazard way, by human beings themselves. Not all human controls have been good. Tyrants such as Hitler and Stalin have been able to manipulate the collective behavior of an entire nation through a combination of physical and psychological threats against the individual. No one can yet be sure that a new tyrant, equipped now with nuclear arms, will not be able to manipulate the collective behavior of the whole world.

Because the technological development of human society rests more and more on the invention and use of machines, man has come to depend more and more on what machines tell him to do. Indeed, machines may mean the difference between life and death for many who live in technologically developed countries. The complex system by which the earth is planted and harvested for food in the United States is more and more dependent on machines, such as planters, cultivators, reapers, harvesters, and food processors. Without the use of such machines, crop yield would be much smaller, perhaps so much less that many would starve to death.

We tend to forget our dependence on the machine for food, clothing, shelter, communication, and transportation, but we seldom are without some kind of mechanical device and often so dependent on it that we do not think about it. Few civilized men, for example, can ignore the ringing of a telephone. They have become so conditioned to its ring that they have a compulsion to answer it, even if it is not their phone.

The world is filled with devices more complicated and with an even greater impact on man's life than the telephone. Television now reaches into the majority of homes in the United States and Europe and is an important way of sending information to everyone. Cheap transistor radios, most of them made in Japan, have had much the same result in Southeast Asia. Information can be both given and withheld from men's minds on a scale never before known. The sum of technology in communications is to expand the ways in which man's behavior can be manipulated and, at the same time, to concentrate in the hands of fewer and fewer persons the control of the machines that convey information.

This ability to disseminate mass information is at once man's greatest hope and greatest fear. The hope is that it will lead to better understanding between individuals. The fear is embodied in such a novel as *1984* by George Orwell. In *1984*, television works not only to spread information, but also to assemble it. It pries into every room, leaving almost no place hidden from the sight of an unseen dictator named Big Brother. Through this system Big Brother, who may or may not exist—it is never clear —controls all thought and all individual action.

It is not yet 1984, and its nightmare society has not yet come to the world. Yet it could. As man struggles with forces that may make it happen, he is tossed between a brighter future than he has ever known and the control of himself by those he does not know.

10

Four Billion Astronauts

Man has embarked on two great voyages. One is outward beyond the earth into the infinity of space, to the stars, to other worlds, in search of other life. The second is inward into the recesses of his own mind. The destination in both journeys is unknown, the way to both goals is unclear, the means to both final ports of call have not yet been devised.

This book has been concerned with man's second journey, the voyage into his own mind and body, and with the ways by which he may accomplish it. It has ignored, for the most part, the search among the stars for other beings similar to himself.

All mankind is concerned with both explorations because our earth is really a spaceship, a mote of dust flung into the universe from a point in time and space that we will never know, toward a destination that none of us living today will ever see. We are the crew of our spaceship, almost four billion of us, and we are protected against the hostile forces beyond the earth by only a thin film of water and air. Except for a few hundred pounds of the moon's surface brought back by astronauts and the burned and broken fragments of occasional meteorites, all that the earth ever was, it is now; all that it is now, it is likely to remain so long as man survives.

The earth, however, will change, as it has changed in the past. Its rocks and water and life will be transformed, reworked into new combinations, and moved by the physical forces of the universe into something different. Change is the key to the universe, and the world will never be precisely the same as it is today. Evolution is not static; it does not stand still. Man is only the most recent of life's forms; he may not be the last. His goal must be to ensure that he does not make his time on earth the final chapter in the history of our planet.

The survival of man, perhaps even the survival of life on earth, is dependent on how well man learns to control himself. The success of his voyage to the stars also depends on the success of his inner exploration. It depends on how we use the limited supplies we carry with us through the sea of space.

Unlike the astronauts we have sent to the moon, we yet have little control over the crew of spaceship Earth. We do not yet control our numbers or the rate at which we are consuming the irreplaceable resources of our planet. Even as our supplies dwindle and our crew grows in size, some of its members are sick and dying. Others argue over how we are to share what remains for us all. Often it seems as if no one cares what happens to the ship or how the voyage continues. Even among the more enlightened members of the crew, no one is sure of survival, for there is no certainty either from the stars or the earth that man was meant to live as a species forever. The earth's past history offers no such hope. Its only record is in the fossils of those species that have gone before us into extinction, in the remains of life forms tried by nature and found wanting.

Yet, at the same time, the earth's past tells us that life is powerful and long-lasting, that for millions of years it has triumphed over the most difficult of conditions, forever reproducing itself and changing, forever reaching toward the stars, as if it knew where it was bound. This great strength of life offers man his only real hope.

The successful survival of a species depends on harmony and control. The life forms that have lived the longest on earth, with the best hope of survival, are those species that have learned to get along with the forces and organisms around them. They neither control nor dominate the world; instead, they have adapted to it.

Man has not fully appreciated this. All too often in the past he has treated spaceship Earth as his private preserve, hacking and grinding up its treasures, spewing them out as if they came from a bottomless barrel of plenty. Man has slaughtered weaker species into extinction. He has respected no other life form, not even his own, seemingly unaware that where his civilizations have collapsed, often it has been because he has failed to respect nature.

Dimly man has begun to see that it is *he* who carries the seeds of his own destruction; it is *he* who must learn to save himself; it is *he* who must know his own limits. If nothing else, the past shows man that he must learn and respect natural laws; he is not exempt from nature or superior to it; he, too, is unable to escape the consequences of refusing to obey its rules.

Other species also have made mistakes in the past. As René J. Dubos, a famous scientist and writer, has said, "Nature by itself is incapable of fully expressing the diversified potentialities of the earth."

The problem man faces, however, will not be solved

by a "return to nature." Retreat to the caves and lakesides from which he emerged ten thousand years ago will not save him. The technological civilization he has created and through which he has exerted his domination over the world cannot and should not be dismantled. Abandoning cities for a grim survival as a creature only a step or two removed from bare existence will not ensure his continued life. Indeed, such action might well bring his extinction. To return to nature would not only be several steps backward into time, it might also doom much of nature. Other species are now dependent on man.

Man must humanize the earth; he must learn to live *in* nature, rather than *in spite* of it. The difference between man *in* nature and man *and* nature is what this book is about. Man has exerted his rule of the earth through his brain. That rule has not been order. To achieve order, man must extend the use of his brain to control both himself and the natural world.

Such control will not be easily won. Man remains somewhere between animal and angel, a creature unlike any other that has inhabited the earth. His brain has given him domination of the planet; it has not yet given him control of himself. Control of anything implies using less than the full amount of power available, something man has not been able to do. Yet he cannot control the earth if he burns all the energy it possesses. Nor can he achieve a climax community if he reproduces himself to the greatest number of humans possible. He can achieve a balanced world only if he learns respect for other forms of life.

Control also implies that power must be concentrated and directed toward a goal. It requires conforming to rules to conserve energy and keeping population equal to the land space and food resources available. Too often man has believed the earth is his for the taking. Now he must realize that freedom, like the world, has its limits. True freedom carries with it heavy responsibility—responsibility not only for himself, but also for other species. Freedom is not the right to do completely as one wishes; rather it is a privilege, the privilege to life itself. Because all life on earth is related, and because man is only the latest expression of the long chain of events that began with the formation of the first molecule of DNA, man is the present guardian of life. If he is to guarantee both his own survival and the survival of life on this planet, he must also be its conservator.

This sense of responsibility has been called *bioethics*, a combination of biological knowledge and human values. Bioethics includes many of the things already discussed in this book:

—Population control: the use of artificial contraception and abortion, sperm banks, and laws regulating the size of families.

—Genetic control and engineering: the alteration of genes, the use of chemistry, physics, and biology to control the future of Homo sapiens.

—Behavior control: the regulation of the mind and brain through behavior modification, electrical brain stimulation, conditioning, and other, as yet undiscovered, ways of affecting the way we think and act.

—Diet control: the addition and subtraction of vital elements in our most precious source of energy, food.

—Pollution control: the effective reduction of pollution of the biosphere by man's machines and by man himself.

—Energy control: the conservation of fossil fuels, the search for new sources of plentiful power.

—Control and extension of life through transplantation and artificial organs.

In each of these areas man faces great unknowns. With each he can make profound changes both in himself and in the world. Just as technology gave man the tools with which to begin the Industrial Revolution, so will the new revolution in bioethics create an earth far different from the one we now know. It remains for man to decide whether the world will be a better or worse place in which to live.

In embarking on his inner voyage, in beginning the bioethical revolution, man may well be tampering with the most powerful life force on earth, evolution itself. Evolution has both order and control. If man looks back over the millions of years of evolution, he sees that life has evolved both in amount and complexity. Where the earth was once barren of life, it now abounds with millions of species. These species have grown in complexity with the length of evolution. At the same time, evolution seems to be shortening the time in which new species are developed, almost as if it were more certain with each new creature that appears. The age of dinosaurs was millions of years in length; the evolution of mammals has been much shorter; man's development has come in even less time. In the space of a few milliseconds in the long-time scale of life on this planet, man has burst upon the world and overwhelmed it, altering its surface, dominating all other species and controlling all other animals. Can he now control himself? Is he the final answer to evolution? Can he so modify himself through his brain, an organ without equal among all other species, that he, too, will live for millions of years?

The greatest times in man's history have been those

when the human spirit was uplifted by a new vision of his place in the universe. The men who emerged from the world of ice to settle by the Tigris and Euphrates rivers saw beyond the cold to a new world filled with growing crops. Moses brought law and a single God to the earth. Jesus described for man a society in which all men are brothers. Copernicus saw the globe for what it really is, a minor planet revolving around the sun. Darwin brought order into the confusion and profusion of life. Einstein saw that all the universe is related, no matter how great it is or how far it extends.

In this century man has, for the first time, escaped the earth and gone to the moon. Through cameras on other spacecraft he has been able to look upon the surface of another planet, Mars. Thus he has embarked on the first of his two great voyages. But he looks inward, too, toward a horizon that is much nearer, yet more distant than space. He gazes upon that scene with awe, and he wonders if he is equal to the vision before him.

Bibliography

Asimov, Isaac, *The Bloodstream*, New York, Macmillan, 1961.
———, *Intelligent Man's Guide to the Biological Sciences*, New York, Washington Square Press, 1968.
———, *Life and Energy*, New York, Avon, 1972.
———, *The Wellsprings of Life*, New York, New American Library, 1960.
Bates, Marston, *The Forest and the Sea*, New York, Random House, 1960.
Carrington, Richard, *A Million Years of Man*, New York, New American Library, 1964.
Chasteen, Edgar R., *The Case for Compulsory Birth Control*, Englewood Cliffs, N. J., Prentice-Hall, 1971.
Control of the Mind, A Symposium, New York, McGraw-Hill, 1960.
Corporation and a Molecule, A, Palo Alto, Calif., Syntex Laboratories, undated.
Curtis, Helena, *The Viruses*, New York, Natural History Press, 1965.
Eiseley, Loren, *The Invisible Pyramid*, New York, Charles Scribner, 1970.
Farb, Peter, and the editors of *Life*, *Ecology*, New York, Time-Life Books, 1963.
Hardin, Clifford H., *Overcoming World Hunger*, Englewood Cliffs, N. J., Prentice-Hall, 1969.
Hardin, Garrett, *Birth Control*, New York, Western Books Publishers, 1970.
London, Perry, *Behavior Control*, New York, Harper and Row, 1969.
MacGowan, Kenneth, and Hester, Joseph A., *Early Man in the New World*, New York, Natural History Press, 1962.
Mercer, Edgar H., *Cells, Their Structure and Function*, revised edition, New York, Natural History Press, 1967.

Michelmore, Susan, *Sexual Reproduction,* New York, Natural History Press, 1964.

Moore, Francis, *Give and Take,* New York, Doubleday, 1965.

Pohlman, Edward, *How to Kill Population,* Philadelphia, Westminster Press, 1961.

Rapport, Samuel, and Wright, Helen, eds., *The Crust of the Earth, An Introduction to Geology,* New York, Signet Science Library, 1955.

Read, John, *A Direct Entry into Organic Chemistry,* New York, Harper and Row, 1960.

Rosenfeld, Albert, *The Second Genesis, The Coming Control of Life,* New York, Arena Books, 1972.

The Scientific Endeavor, New York, The Rockefeller Institute Press, undated.

Tyler, Edward T., ed., *Birth Control, A Continuing Controversy,* Springfield, Ill., Charles C Thomas, 1967.

Watson, James D., *Molecular Biology of the Gene,* New York, W. A. Benjamin, 1965.

Index

A

Abortion and contraception, 136

Abstract thought as a human characteristic, 22

Acids, nucleic, 69

Action therapy for mental illness, 154

Adaptation. *See also* Evolution.
  as a life characteristic, 17
  of life forms and DNA, 86
  and mutation, 36
  and sexual reproduction, 36
  and survival, 167

Adrenaline, discovery of, 70

Afferent nerve cells, 55

Agriculture
  and the destruction of the Great Plains, 28
  and human life-styles, 24

Alteration of living molecules, 67

Amino acids, 37
  and codons, 77, 79
  relationship to proteins and genes, 73

Amphibians, evolution of, 39

Animals

Animals
  controlled reproduction of, 103
  sperm banks for, 104
  superovulation of, 104

Antibodies, 38, 87

Antigens, 38, 87

Artificial
  blood vessels, 95
  conception of humans, 101, 107
  contraception, 134
  heart, possibilities for, 97
  insemination, animal, 104
  insemination, human, 107
  kidney, 91
  man, 98
  mutations of fruit flies, 73
  organs, use of, 94
  parts, prolongation of life with, 98

Asexual reproduction, 106

Australopithecus, 21

Automobile pollution, 129

B

Balance
  of life processes, 16
  of nature and species, 13

174

Prenatal
  immunity, 90
  life, control of, 101
  testing for genetic defects,
    111
Primates, 20
  early, 21
  and man, 20
Progesterone
  , action of, 133
  production from yams, 131
Prolongation of life with
    artificial parts, 98
Protein
  , amino acids, and genes,
    relationship between,
    73
  , differentiation of, 38
  , formation of, 37
  hormones, 70
  , study of, 71
  synthesis, 36
  synthesis and codons, 79
  synthesis and Mattahei, 78
Psychoanalysis, 149

R

Races of mankind, 47
Radioactive elements as
    energy sources, 123
Receptor sites for neurons, 55
Recessive hereditary
    characteristics, 42
Recycling waste, 128
Red blood cells, 87

Redwoods, importance to
    science of, 13
  See also Sequoia.
Rejection
  and immunity, transplant,
    88
  and skin grafts, 89
Remaking man, necessity for,
    130
Repair of body, control of
    life through, 86
Replacements
  for heart parts, 96
  for humans, machine, 98
  , organic, 99
  , plastic ear, 95
Replication, 34. See also
    Reproduction.
Reproduction, 17
  and adaptation, sexual, 36
  , asexual, 106
  , cell, 34
  and cell fusion, 105
  in the climax state, 105
  of conifers, 15
  , controlled human, 103
  as a life characteristic, 17
  of plants and animals,
    controlled, 103
  , sexual, 34
  by vegetative multiplica-
    tion, 105
Research
  on contraception, 141
  methods of science, 64